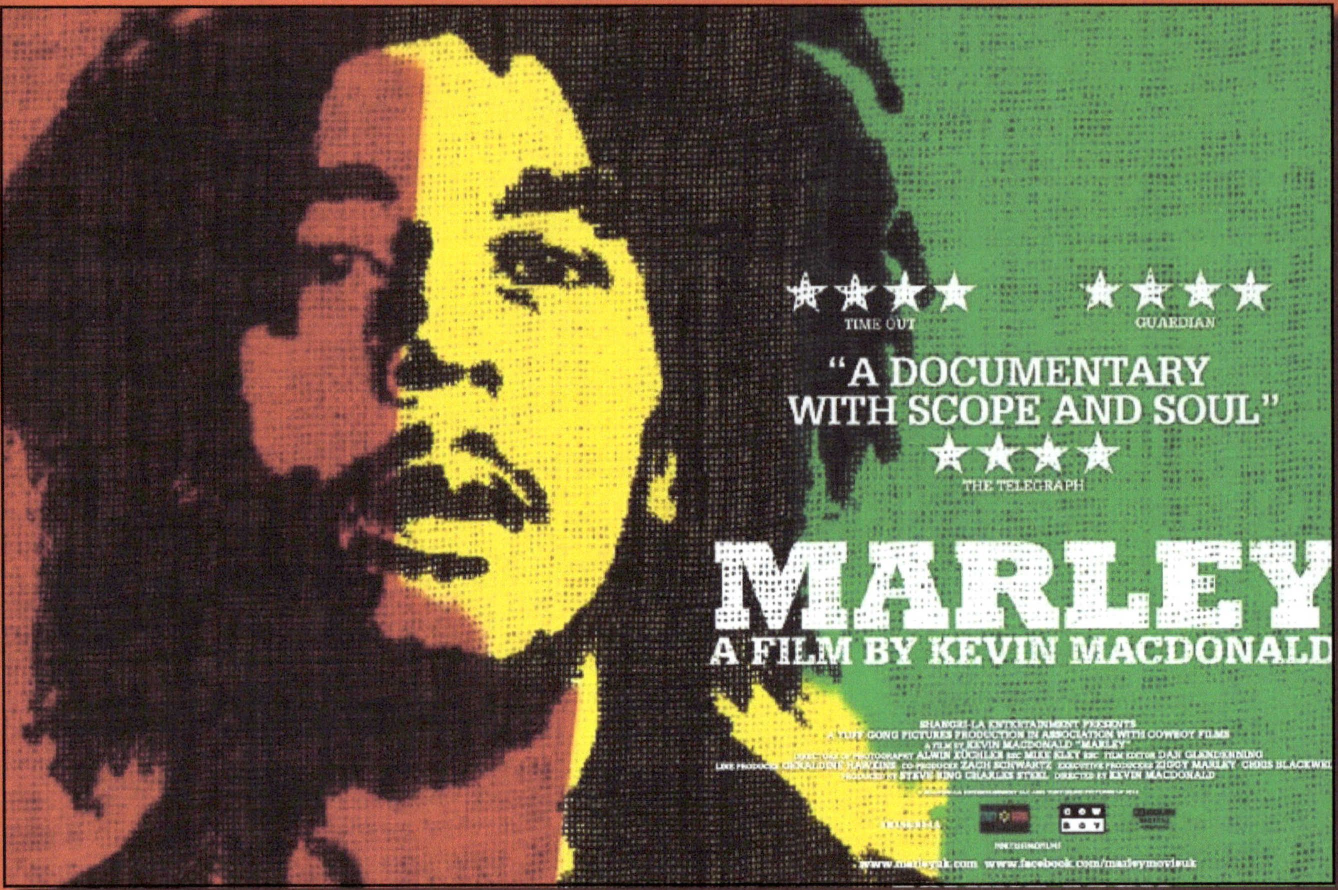

★ ★★★ ★★★★
TIME OUT   GUARDIAN

"A DOCUMENTARY
WITH SCOPE AND SOUL"
★★★★
THE TELEGRAPH

MARLEY
A FILM BY KEVIN MACDONALD

SHANGRI-LA ENTERTAINMENT PRESENTS
A TUFF GONG PICTURES PRODUCTION IN ASSOCIATION WITH COWBOY FILMS
A FILM BY KEVIN MACDONALD "MARLEY"
DIRECTOR OF PHOTOGRAPHY ALWIN KÜCHLER BSC MIKE ELEY BSC FILM EDITOR DAN GLENDENNING
LINE PRODUCER GERALDINE HAWKINS CO-PRODUCER ZACH SCHWARTZ EXECUTIVE PRODUCERS ZIGGY MARLEY CHRIS BLACKWELL
PRODUCED BY STEVE BING CHARLES STEEL DIRECTED BY KEVIN MACDONALD

www.marleyuk.com   www.facebook.com/marleymovieuk

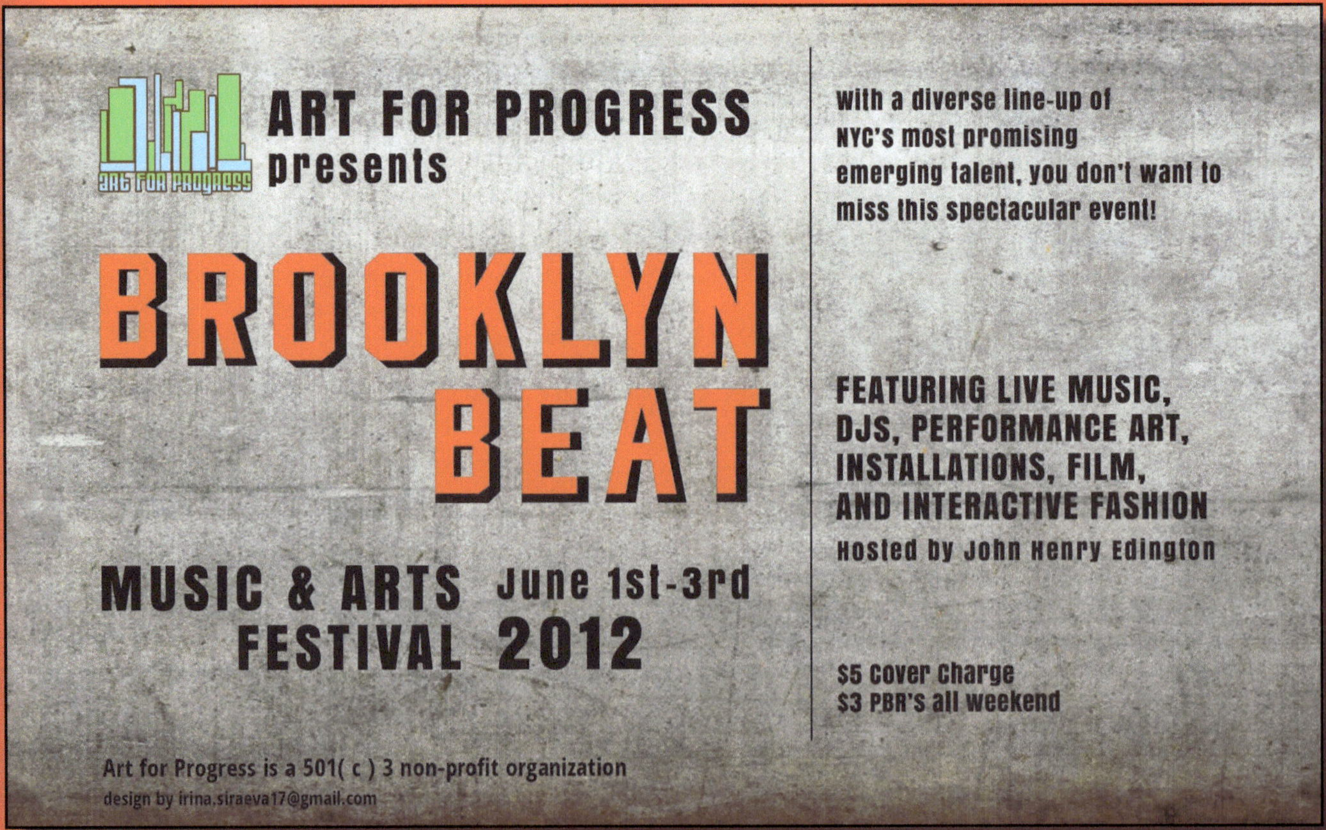

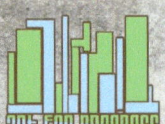

ART FOR PROGRESS
presents

BROOKLYN
BEAT

MUSIC & ARTS
FESTIVAL
June 1st-3rd
2012

with a diverse line-up of
NYC's most promising
emerging talent, you don't want to
miss this spectacular event!

**FEATURING LIVE MUSIC,
DJS, PERFORMANCE ART,
INSTALLATIONS, FILM,
AND INTERACTIVE FASHION**
Hosted by John Henry Edington

$5 Cover Charge
$3 PBR's all weekend

Art for Progress is a 501(c) 3 non-profit organization
design by irina.siraeva17@gmail.com

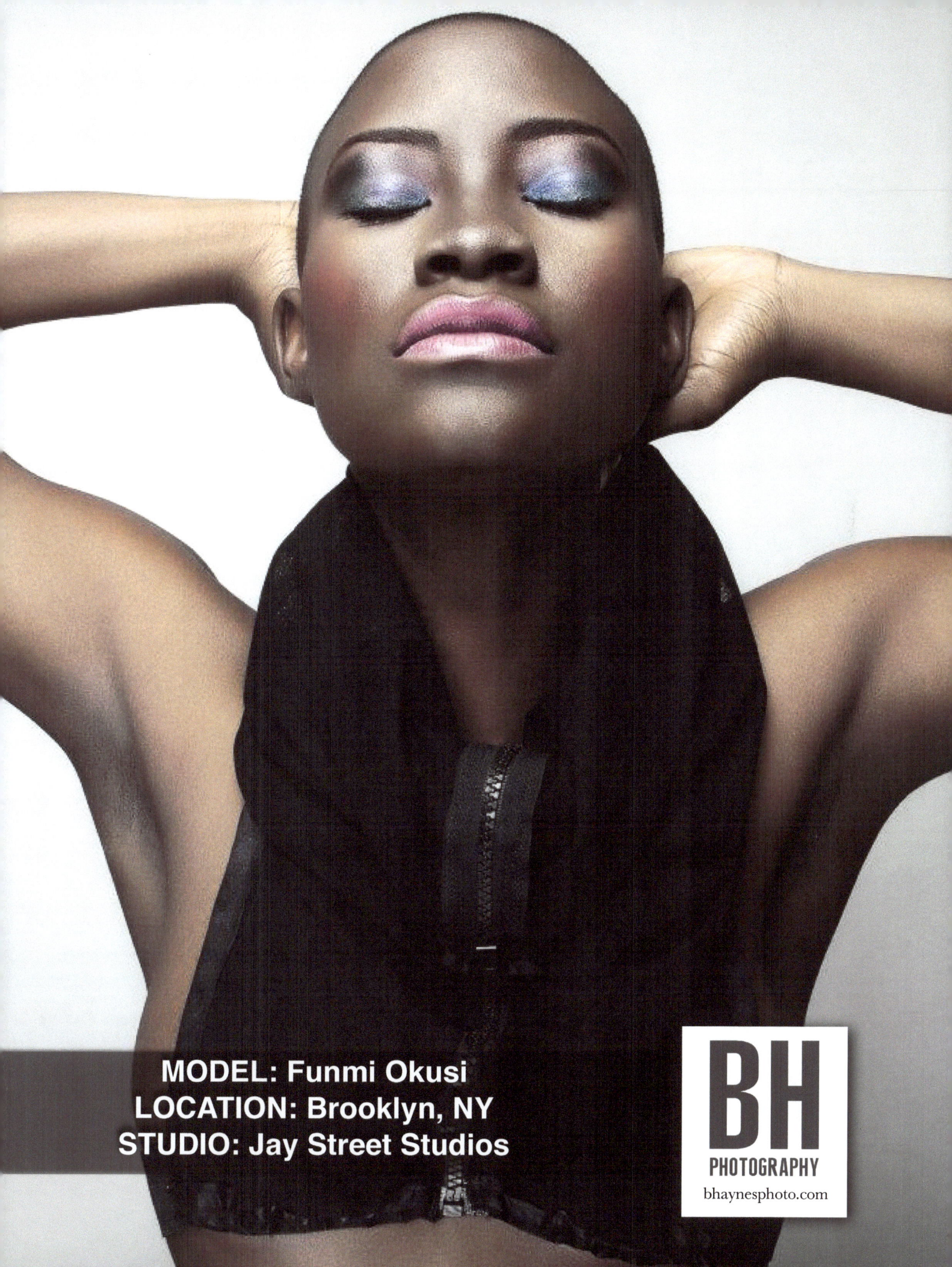

MODEL: Funmi Okusi
LOCATION: Brooklyn, NY
STUDIO: Jay Street Studios

BH
PHOTOGRAPHY
bhaynesphoto.com

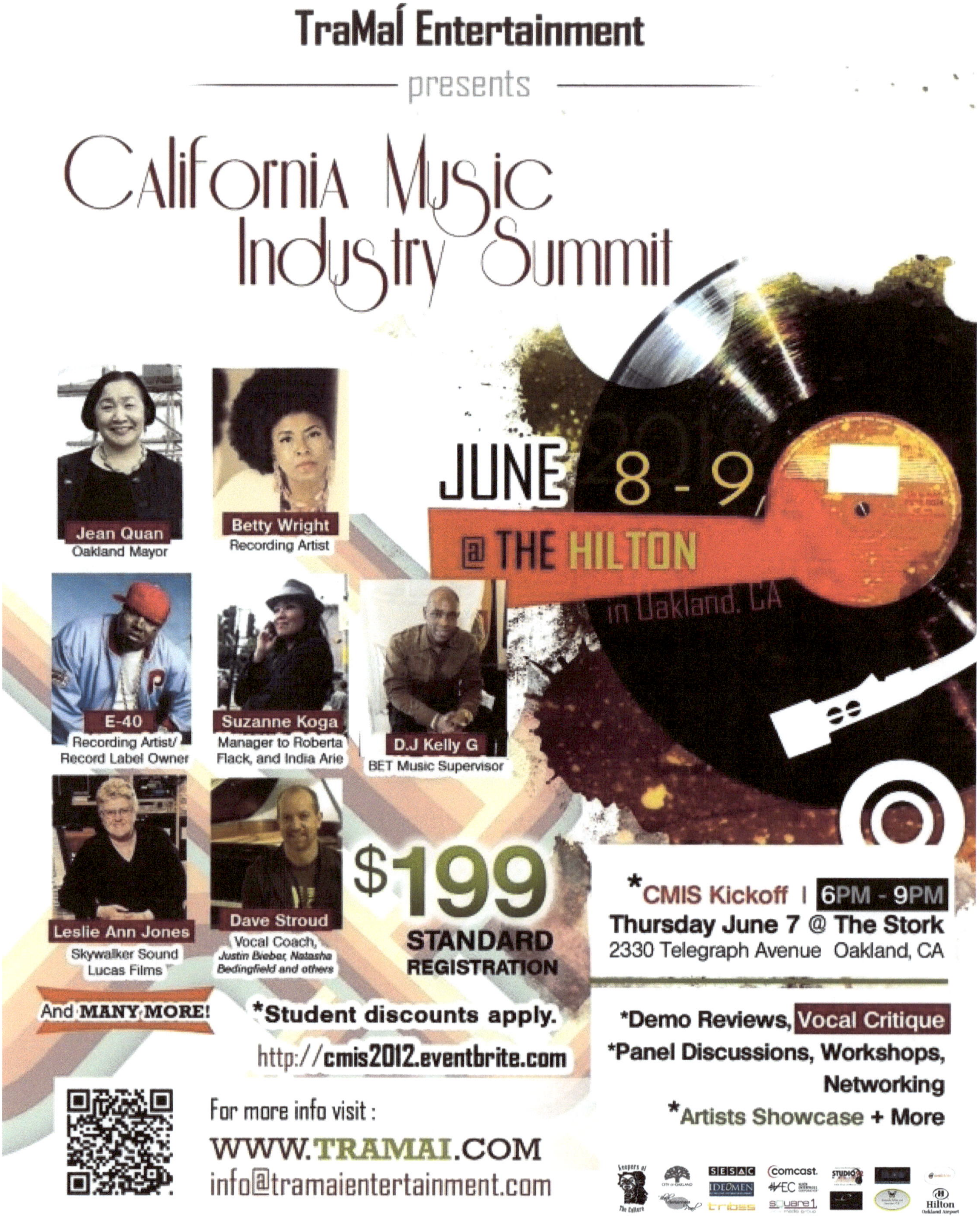

TraMaí Entertainment

presents

California Music Industry Summit

Jean Quan
Oakland Mayor

Betty Wright
Recording Artist

E-40
Recording Artist/
Record Label Owner

Suzanne Koga
Manager to Roberta
Flack, and India Arie

D.J Kelly G
BET Music Supervisor

Leslie Ann Jones
Skywalker Sound
Lucas Films

Dave Stroud
Vocal Coach,
Justin Bieber, Natasha
Bedingfield and others

And **MANY MORE!**

JUNE 8 - 9
@ THE HILTON
in Oakland. CA

$199
STANDARD REGISTRATION

*Student discounts apply.

http://cmis2012.eventbrite.com

*CMIS Kickoff | 6PM - 9PM
Thursday June 7 @ The Stork
2330 Telegraph Avenue Oakland, CA

*Demo Reviews, Vocal Critique
*Panel Discussions, Workshops,
Networking
*Artists Showcase + More

For more info visit :

WWW.TRAMAI.COM
info@tramaientertainment.com

TRIBES MAGAZINE - OFFICIAL 2012 MEDIA SPONSORS

SPARK AFRICA ISSUE!

COVER STORY

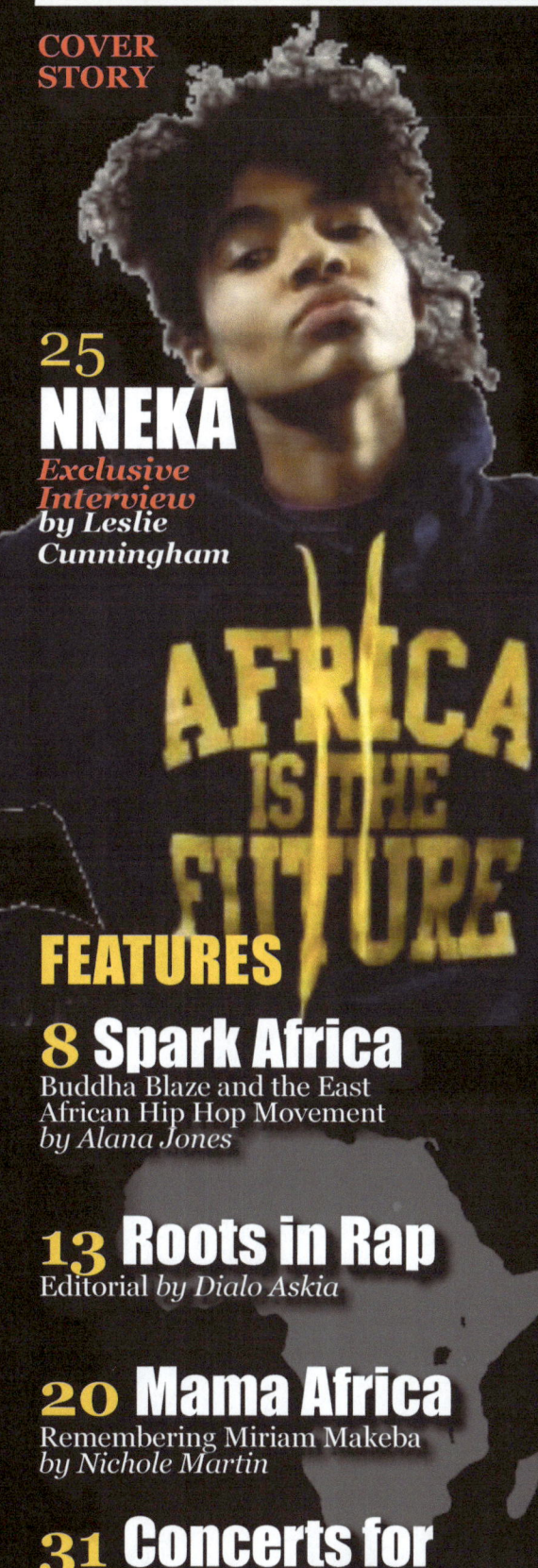

25 NNEKA
Exclusive Interview by Leslie Cunningham

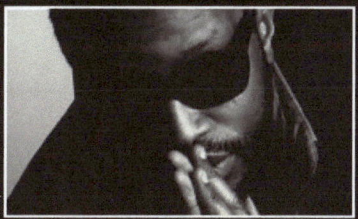
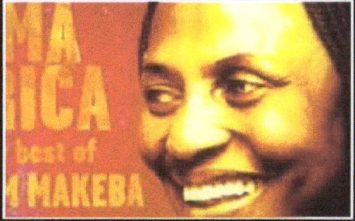
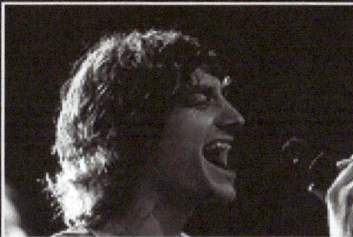
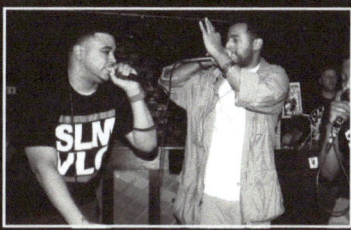
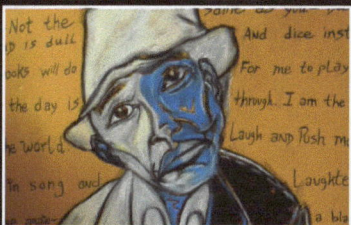
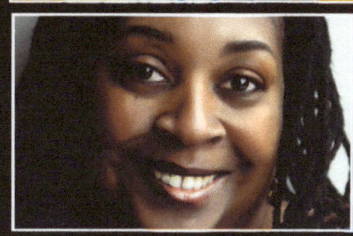
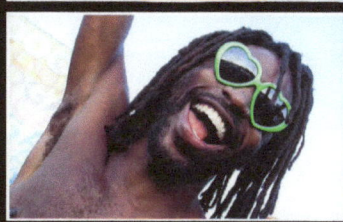

DOWNLOAD NNEKA'S SONG "HEARTBEAT" FREE at tribesmagazine.com

INSIDE TRIBES

Get TRIBES' 2012 **TOP TEN** Summer Concert Picks on Page 35!

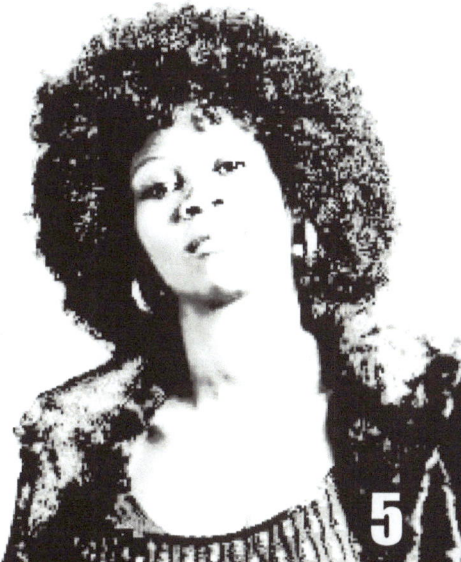

tribes

SUMMER 2012
Issue #35

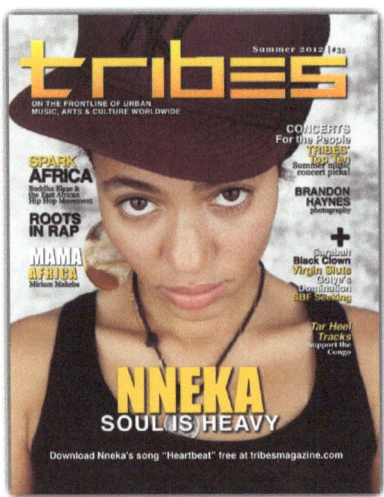

PUBLISHED BY
TRIBES Entertainment

**CREATOR/
EDITOR-IN-CHIEF**
Leslie Cunningham

EXECUTIVE EDITOR
Alana Jones

GRAPHIC DESIGNER
TRIBES Creative Group

PHOTOGRAPHER
Emanuel Cole Studios

EMAIL:
whatsup@tribesmagazine.com

WEBSITES:
tribesmagazine.com
tribesentertainment.com

CONTRIBUTORS

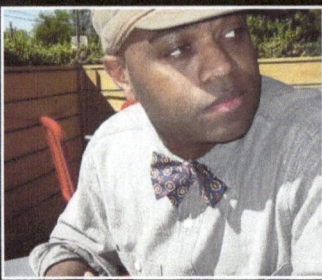

DIALO ASKIA was born in Chicago, IL. The son of teachers, his childhood was a classroom with crayons, pencils, pads, and pens always within arm's reach. His educational endeavors brought him to Clark Atlanta University where he earned a degree in Political Science. Dialo has lent his pen to commentary and various copy, and continues to write about everything under the sun.

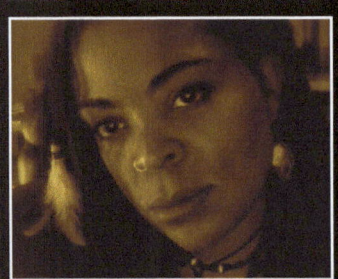

LESLIE CUNNINGHAM is creator and publisher of *TRIBES Magazine*. Originally from Los Angeles, CA, she is a seasoned marketing professional studying documentary film at Duke University's Center for Documentary Studies. A longtime artist, activist and writer, Leslie uses TRIBES to share her love of visual arts, writing and photography.

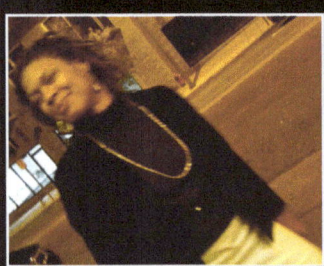

ALANA JONES, a South Orange, New Jersey native, is an entertainment journalist, fiction writer, editor, and cultural anthropologist. A graduate of Duke University, Alana is editor and senior writer for *TRIBES Magazine* as well as contributor for other local publications in North Carolina.

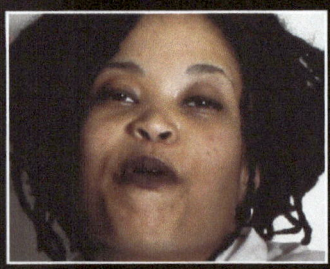

NICHOLE MARTIN has been a senior writer for TRIBES for more than five years. Originally from Akron, Ohio, Nichole now resides in Chapel Hill, North Carolina with her 13 year-old son, Nicholas. She holds a Bachelor's degree in Communications from North Carolina A&T State University and works as a freelance editor. In her spare time, she writes fictional literature.

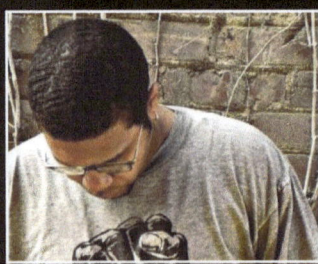

GABRIEL RICH has been a prominent Raleigh voice in both music and sports. As a sports writer, Gabriel covered both high school and college sports as a staff writer for the Raleigh News & Observer, and has also freelanced for TRIBES Magazine, Goldsboro News-Argus, Amsterdam News and Miami Herald.

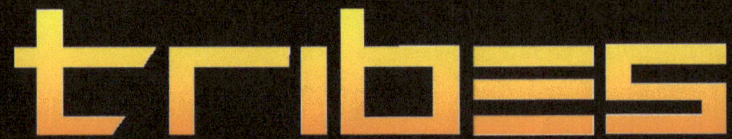

tribes

TRIBES Magazine is always seeking writers, artists, photographers and musicians who are interested in showcasing their work. We are also seeking entertainment journalists to join our team. Email us today at whatsup@tribesmagazine.com.

VISIT TRIBESMAGAZINE.COM

Text by Alana Jones, TRIBES Editor

Editor's Intro

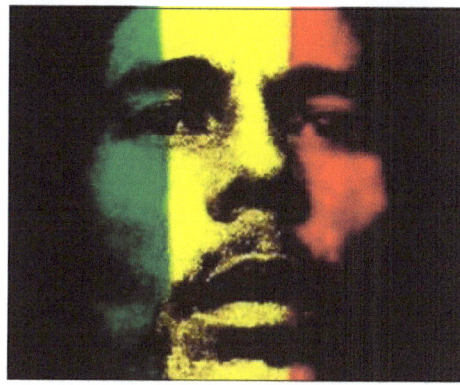

SPARK AFRICA

In the spirit of ushering in a new summer and preparing to bring this latest **TRIBES Magazine Summer 2012**: **Spark Africa** issue to press, the crew at TRIBES Central took a field trip to the Carolina Theatre for a highly anticipated, limited screening of **Marley**, the new documentary film from Kevin MacDonald chronicling the complete life and works of the international superstar. Immersing his art in the political and socioeconomic realities of life in post-colonial Jamaica and committed to reclaiming a cultural homeland and spiritual roots for all members of the **Africa diaspora**, Bob Marley was beloved by his fans and peers for his commitment to the work of truth and reconciliation in his music and the love for humanity that permeated his life and work.

In this issue of *TRIBES Magazine*, join us as we head to Nigeria, Kenya, Sierra Leon, Guinea Bissau, Senegal, and S. Africa by way of Germany and the United States, to meet musician and activist **Nneka**- raising awareness around big oil business, natural resource exploitation, and state corruption in her hometown of Warri- Hip Hop Activist, promoter,

and journalist, **Buddha Blaze**- co-founder of Spark Africa and various efforts to generate and unify Hip Hop communities across the African continent- **Sister Fa**- Female MC and subject of the new documentary film, *Sarabah*, on her mission to combat female genital mutilation (FGM) practices in her Senegalese homeland- and MAMA AFRICA, **Miriam Makeba**, and her peace and humanitarian work during and after the fall of apartheid in her native South Africa.

These individuals, and the other artists and activists to grace the pages of this Spark Africa edition, teach us that through intensely personal, substantively relevant expressions of art and culture, we become infinitely connected and limitless beings with voices amplified for the work of improving our world. Celebrate inspired community and the arts with our favorite summer concerts and festivals, write your Spark Africa summer playlist after a visit to our Music TRIBES and find inspiration for new forms of expression in **Pierce Freelon's** latest project, *Tar Heel Tracks*, and **Renaldo Davidson's** collaborative, mixed-media work, *Black Clown*.

In this summer of 2012, love, and as a means for revolution, reigns supreme and thus, we welcome you to the TRIBES Magazine 2012: SPARK AFRICA Issue.

May your heart's light illuminate the darkness!

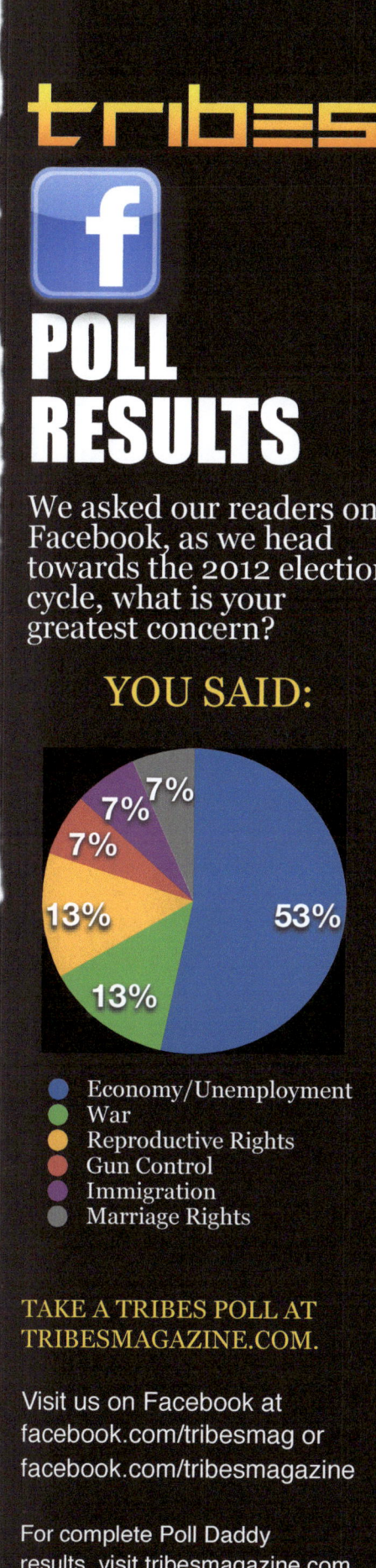

tribes

POLL RESULTS

We asked our readers on Facebook, as we head towards the 2012 election cycle, what is your greatest concern?

YOU SAID:

53%

13%

13%

7%

7%

7%

7%

- ● Economy/Unemployment
- ● War
- ● Reproductive Rights
- ● Gun Control
- ● Immigration
- ● Marriage Rights

TAKE A TRIBES POLL AT TRIBESMAGAZINE.COM.

Visit us on Facebook at facebook.com/tribesmag or facebook.com/tribesmagazine

For complete Poll Daddy results, visit tribesmagazine.com.

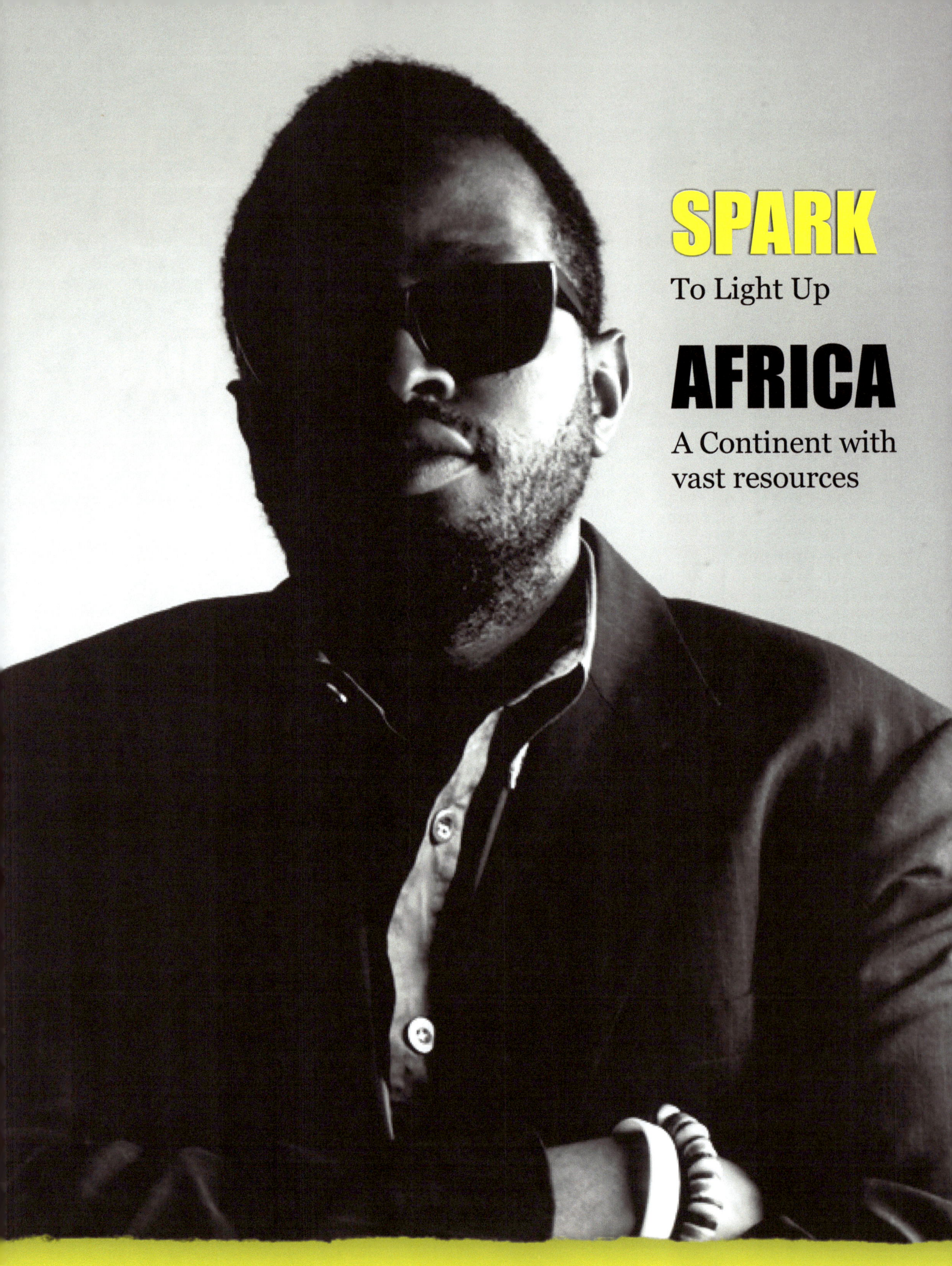

SPARK

To Light Up

AFRICA

A Continent with
vast resources

Text by Alana Jones.
Photographs compliments of Spark Africa.

Feature Story

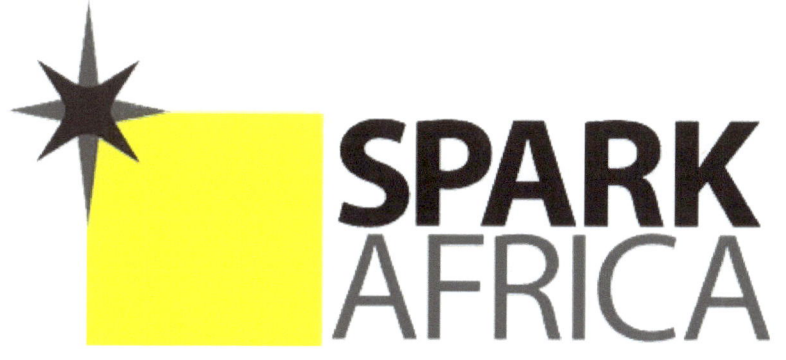

SPARK AFRICA: BUDDHA BLAZE

AND THE EAST AFRICAN HIP HOP MOVEMENT

Buddha Blaze has been building a home for Hip Hop in Kenya and bridging markets across the Motherland for some time. Touting a career resume in the arena of music entertainment, jam packed with groundbreaking moments in **African Hip Hop**, Buddha Blaze has helped to generate the growing wave of rhymes from the original underground. Thus, we introduce you, TRIBES readers and family, to Buddha Blaze, our TRIBES in Nairobi correspondent and connection to one of the world's next and most exciting popular music and culture movements.

Buddha Blaze's media coverage of his Hip Hop community coupled with his entertainment production projects, and contributions to the movement of Hip Hop music and culture, more generally, have taken all variety of forms. Creative partner of *Spark Africa,* a multi-media authority on African urban culture and entertainment, Buddha Blaze is also founder of *Slam Africa*, Kenya's premier poetry event and creator of Kenya's first hip-hop website, **kenyanhiphop.com**. Former editor and writer for East Africa's first entertainment periodical, *PHAT! Magazine*

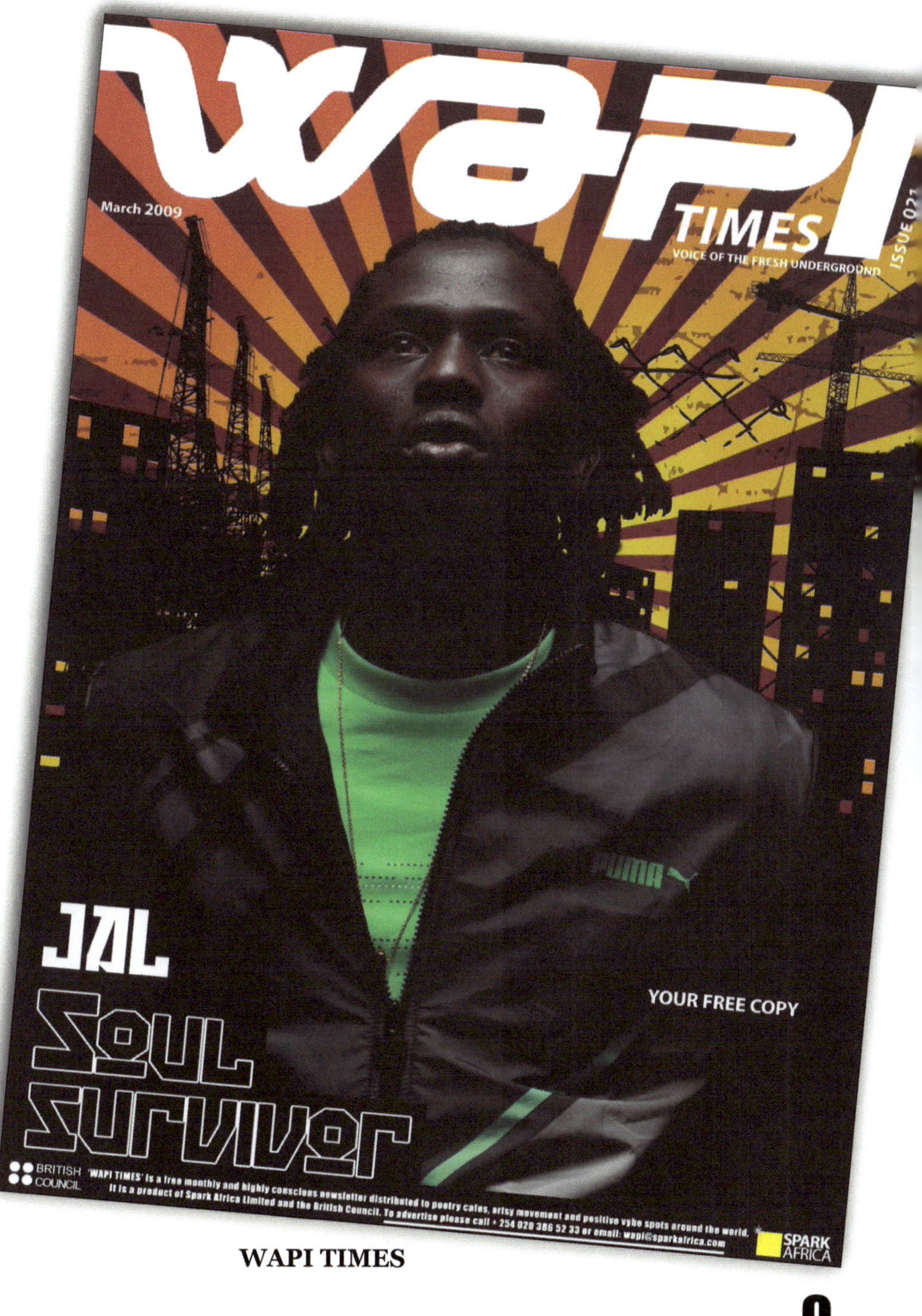

WAPI TIMES

9

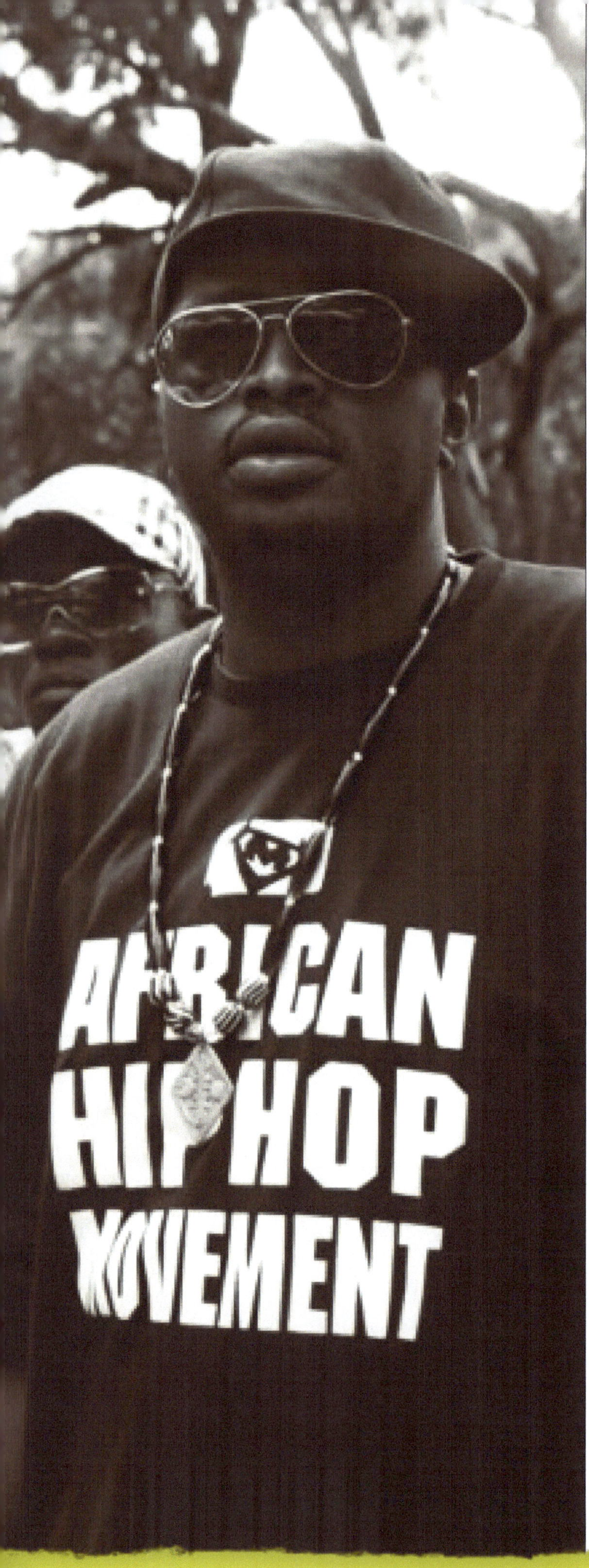

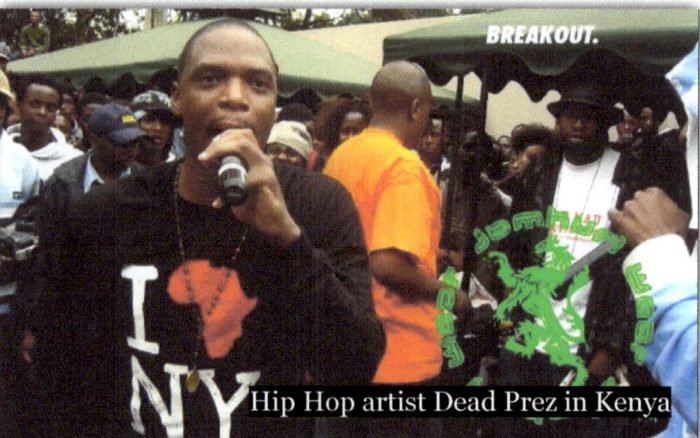
Hip Hop artist Dead Prez in Kenya

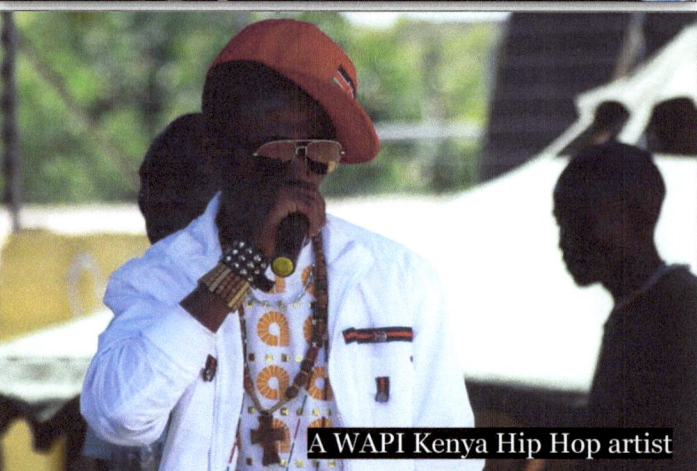
A WAPI Kenya Hip Hop artist

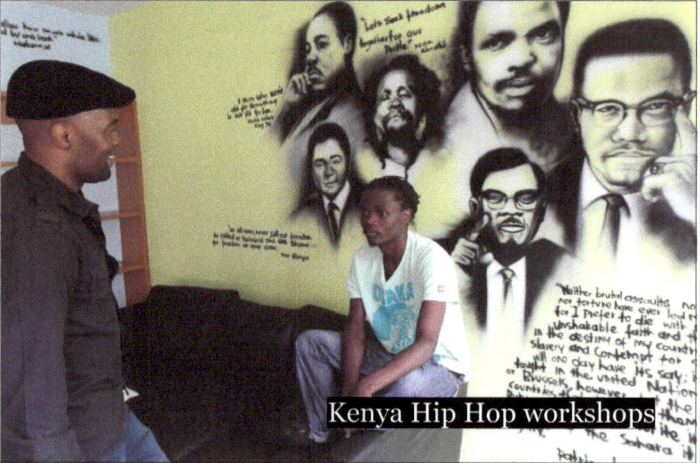
Kenya Hip Hop workshops

and coordinator of the Spark Africa-managed **WAPI (*Words and Pictures*)**, a global artists' movement, Buddha Blaze is a Hip Hop activist with a passion for global art, culture and music.

Committed to providing a platform on this world stage for budding African artists, Buddha Blaze has successfully elevated Hip Hop music to new levels in Kenya and helped shine a spotlight on African artists before world audiences. In 2002, Buddha Blaze spearheaded a mass media campaign to have local radio stations play music by Kenyan artists. The result was an explosion of national and regional recognition for local artists and

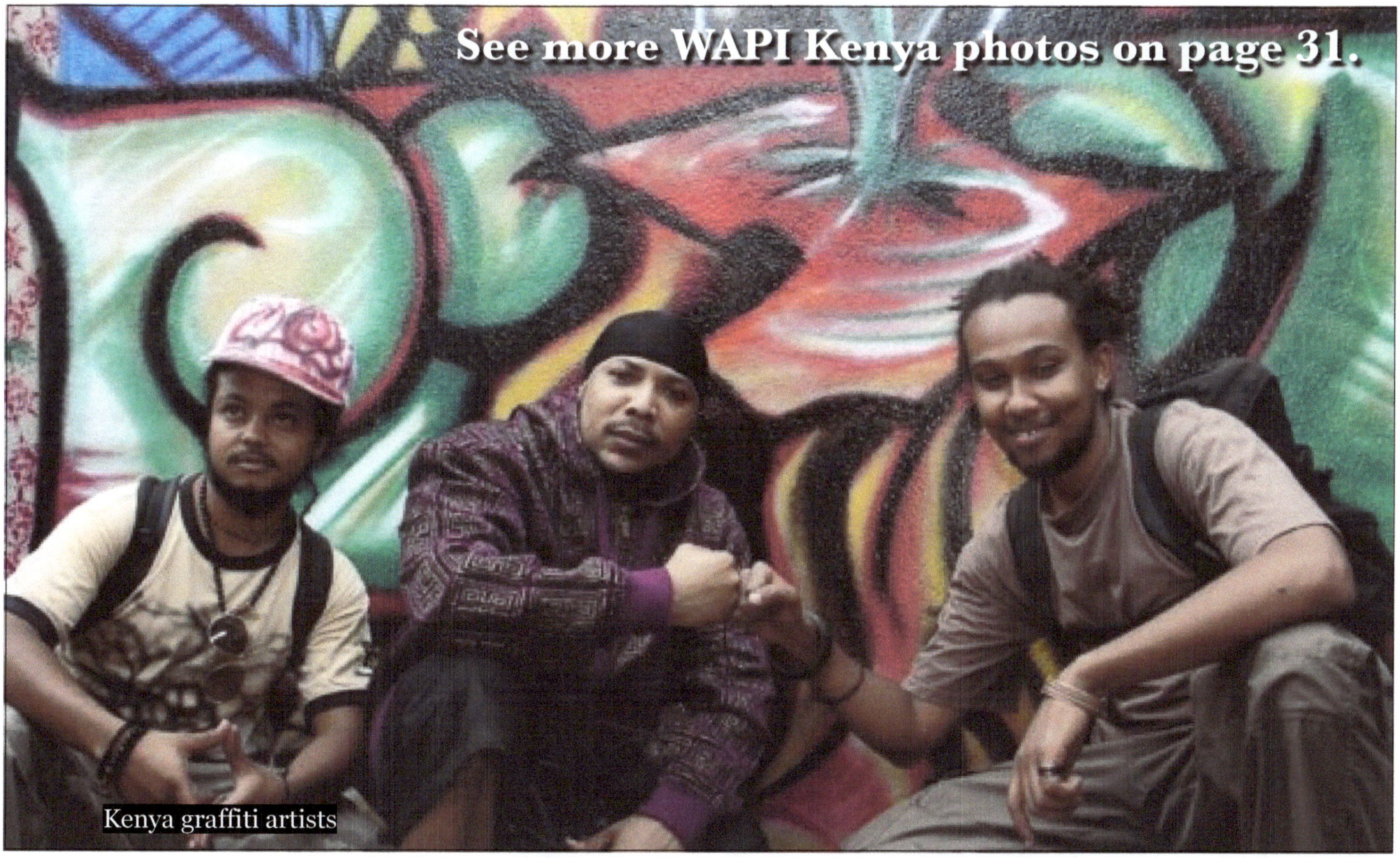

See more WAPI Kenya photos on page 31.

Kenya graffiti artists

an opportunity for young Kenyan's and Hip Hop heads in the region to hear themselves and their brand of Hip Hop music on the radio. Buddha Blaze also led the first group of Kenyan artists to the **KORA All African Music Awards** in Johannesburg, South Africa in 2003.

"Hip-hop has always had a positive influence on the youth from the urban centers of the world," says Buddha Blaze as he mentions some of the artists to play WAPI stage, including **Dead Prez, Blak Twang,** and **Kamau**. Blaze has also taken WAPI events on the road, sponsoring concert festivals in Nigeria, Ghana, Uganda and Malawi.

Through Spark Africa and his other work, Buddha Blaze has inspired the careers of many African artists and in this

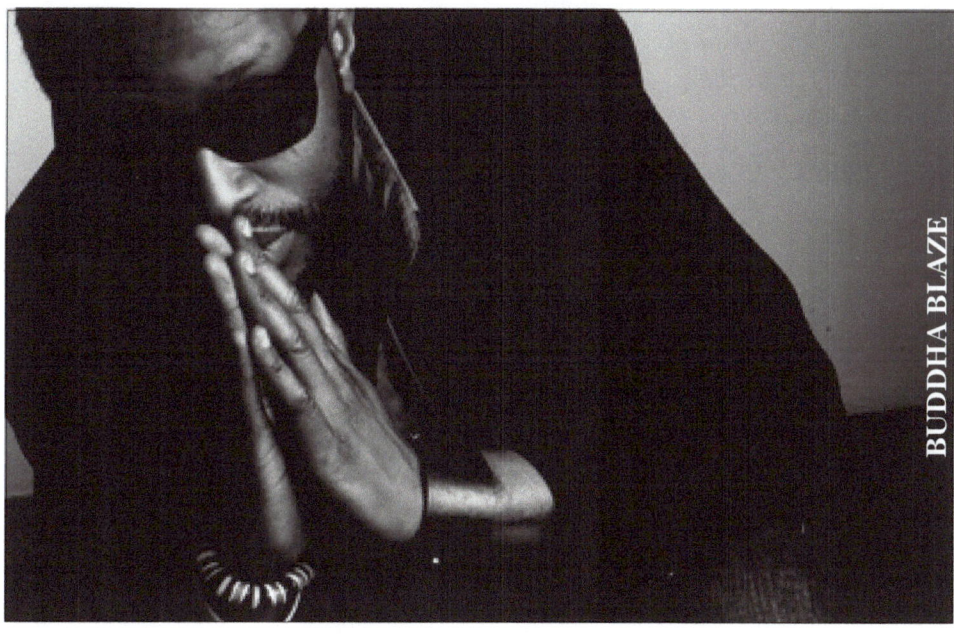

BUDDHA BLAZE

edition of Buddha Blaze on Hip Hop, artists Sauti Sol, Big Mic, Point Blank, Muthoni the Drummer Queen and Liz Ogumbo get a great big TRIBES family shout-out. Give them a listen and **Thanks Buddha for your contributions to TRIBES**. ∎

VISIT Buddha Blaze's blog at buddhablazeworld. blogspot.com.

VISIT SPARK AFRICA facebook.com/sparkafrica facebook.com/wapiweb

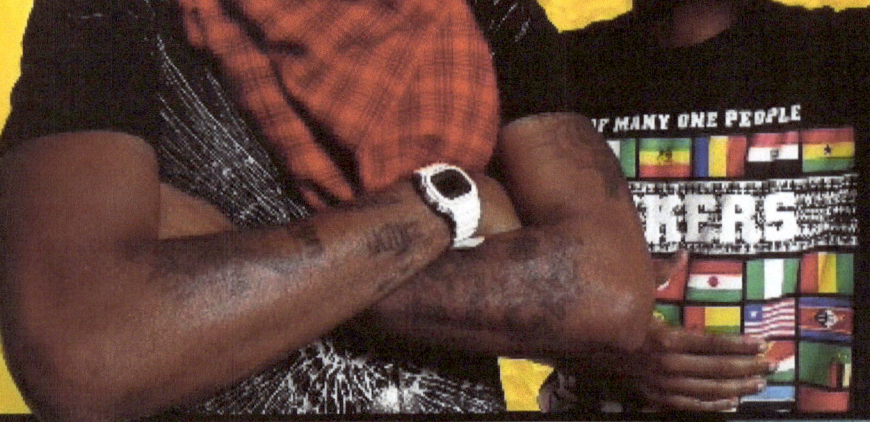
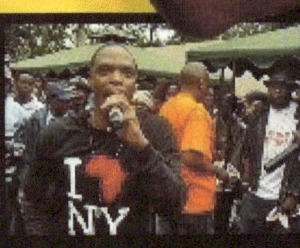

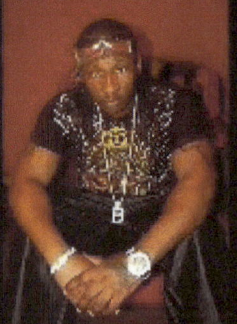
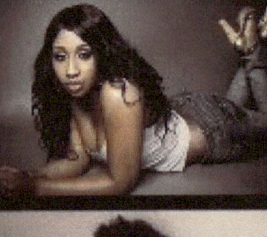
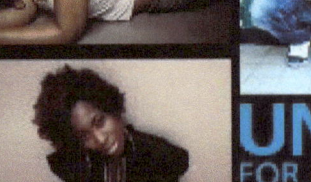
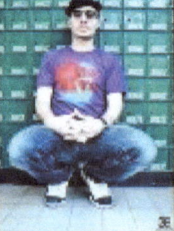
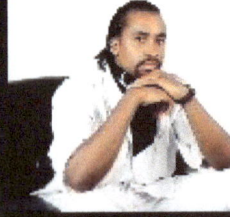

Text by Dialo Askia.
Photographs courtesy of Dialo Askia.

ROOTS IN RAP

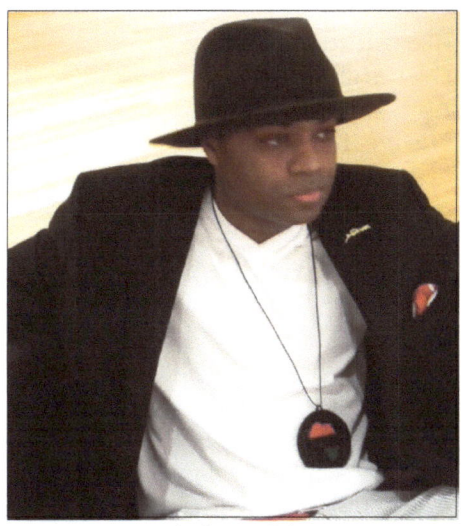

Dialo Askia

Hip Hop started out in the park but if you trace the roots of the Hip Hop tree further, you'll find yourself traveling back through the Caribbean and across the Atlantic to the Motherland, with your ear to the ground, feeling the vibration of the African drum. The early years of Hip Hop held a strong connection to African roots and the music instilled pride in the community while educating listeners.

Greek, Italian, Polish ... my senior year in high school, English class included monthly cultural lessons with visiting college professors that would lead us in study and discussion of various cultures. For the sake of authenticity, professors born of the given culture conducted the lessons and so, on the day of the African studies, I enthusiastically walked to the auditorium ready to be instructed by an academic with roots on African continent, a person of color, only to be greeted by a white professor.

Feeling offended by the fallacy implied- that there were no professors of African descent to speak to us about African culture- I went back to the classroom in protest. My English teacher followed shortly thereafter to encourage me to return to the session. I stood in defiance, labeled a "know-it-all" by my teacher who proffered me a challenge, asking if I could name five African countries. I smirked and in a tempered cadence to mask the melody coming to life in my heart, I recited "**Angola, Soweto, Zimbabwe, Tanzania, Zambia, Mozambique**, and **Botswana**."

I challenged her ignorance and was victorious that day thanks to Stetsasonic and the knowledge they were dropping on tracks like **A.F.R.I.C.A**. And this sort of awareness was not unique to me or other teenage intellectuals and iconoclasts. It was commonplace amongst the youth of my generation.

Feeling offended by the fallacy implied- that there were no professors of African descent to speak to us about African culture- I went back to the classroom in protest.

Hip Hop's emergence coincided with the wave of sociopolitical awareness in the black community that followed the Civil Rights movement and manifested its politic in the rise of Afrocentricity; of styles, ideas, and sound itself. One of the first people to bring this spirit to Hip Hop was the aptly named **Afrika Bambaataa** who along with the Soul Sonic Force hit the charts, the streets, the parks, the clubs, and the radio with the legendary hit classic, Planet Rock.

Afrika Bambaataa put aside his life of gangbanging and created an organization in the 1970's to provide an alternative to the lure of street violence. That organization became the **Universal Zulu Nation** and ignited this new wave of African-centered cultural identification under the crest of a tribal face encircled by the words "Zulu" and "Nation." They dressed in African cultural garb as a show of solidarity with the people living and struggling on the African continent and oppressed people of color around the world and the music, style, and ideas born of Afrika Bambaataa and the Zulu Nation sparked an Afrocentric Hip Hop movement that paved the way for many to follow.

Jungle Brothers' member Afrika Baby Bam (named in honor of Afrika Bambaataa) along with members Mike G and DJ Sammy B invested in the growing movement with songs like Acknowledge Your Own History where Mike G rhymes "I know Afrika's for Afrikans and history's the blood of every woman and man."

Ushering in the "Black Medallion. No gold" transition happening at this moment in Hip Hop, the Jungle Brothers were part of a collective of like-minded, forward thinking, intelligent mc's known as the Native Tongues that also included **De La Soul, A Tribe Called Quest, Queen Latifah,** and Black Sheep. **The Native Tongues** spread the message of awareness in tracks like **De La Soul**'s posse cut Buddy and they imparted the community to take off their gold herringbones and rope chains and put on leather African medallions instead.

However, knowledge of the symbols and their meaning was a prerequisite and across the Hip Hop community, the youth learned to recite 'the red is for the blood. the black is for the man and the green is for the land'. A Tribe Called Quest donned dashikis in their video for the chart-topper "I left my wallet in El Segundo" while Quest member, Jarobi, sports a pyramid pendant. A series of ankhs seperate the words of the Quest logo while **Queen Latifah's** debut album "All Hail the Queen" prominently displays an image of the African continent as Queen poses with the poise her moniker suggests.

Then there was **X-Clan**-the exemplification of Afrocentricism in Hip Hop. Each of their songs was protected by the red, the black, and the green..."with a key!" Their necks were adorned with African beads. Their Funkin' Lesson video featured traditional African dance and while other mc's held mics, **Brother J** delivered his rhymes with a strong grip ever on a tribal staff.

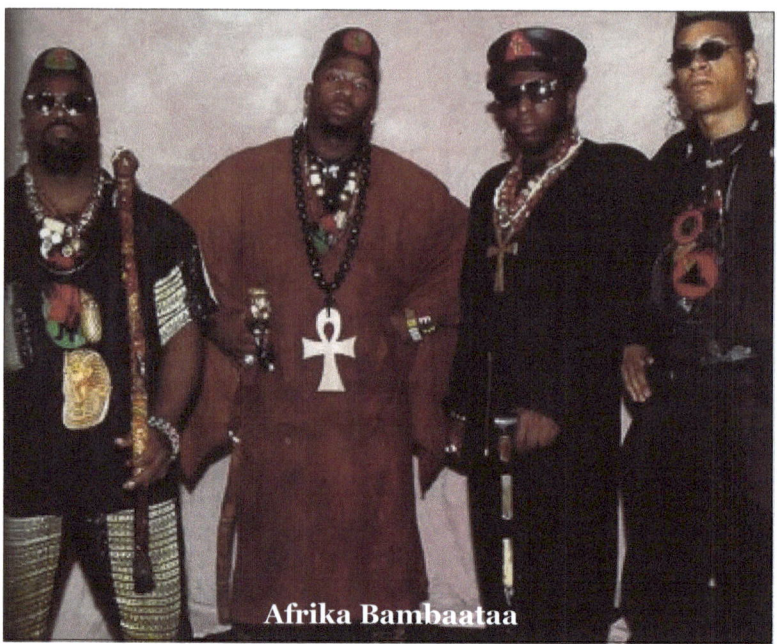

Afrika Bambaataa

They wore leather kufis with ankhs in place of commercial logos.

During this 'Vanglorious' era of Hip Hop, there were a plethora of mc's using their lyrical skills to educate and elevate listeners; and with a broader message about world knowledge and sociopolitical awareness in their music. From the Zulu Nation, Native Tongues, and X-Clan to **Boogie Down Productions, Eric B. and Rakim, Poor Righteous Teachers, Arrested Development**, and **Brand Nubian. Chuck D** of **Public Enemy** had a goal- to inspire 5000 black leaders and It was their "It Takes a Nation..." album that introduced me to South African anti-apartheid activist **Stephen Biko**.

These are not the days of the ignorant rapper. Even braggadocios rappers like Big **Daddy Kane** were much deeper than their surface. (Eager to share the meaning of his name-King Asiatic, Nobody's Equal- he wore a **Nefertiti** medallion on his gold rope and closed out his first classic cd, Long Live the Kane, with the song Word to the Mother (Land)). Irony aside, the

former pimp and hustler turned prime time TV actor, **Ice T**'s "Power" album cover is memorable with a bikini clad girlf posing with a shotgun and Ice wearing an Africa medallion. Unbeknownst to many, Ice T is also a member of the Zulu Nation and his producer Afrika Islam was a protégé of Bambaataa's and DJ of the Zulu Beats show.

This was an era when men in the community greeted each other as brothers and women were treated with respect. Young women and men carried themselves like new-world royalty and knowledge could be heard kicked through headphones, ghetto blasters, and speakers rolling through the streets. Ciphers meant more than just rapping.

Some of our favorite independent artists including Dead Prez, Immortal Technique, Killer Mike, and Gods'illa, carry on the spirit and continue Public Enemy's mission to teach and generate black leaders.

As I finish this article, a rain has started and so I order a pizza. The delivery guy asks 'Is Dialo my last name?' He tells me that the name derives from West Africa and more specifically, the Fulani Tribe, marked by four traditional surnames including my own and his family name, Bah. He talks to me about Sierra Leone and the slave trade and, in spite of the research I've done on my name in my lifetime, I learned something new in the time it takes to listen to a Top 40 Hip Hop track. Let us speak more about the motherland. ∎

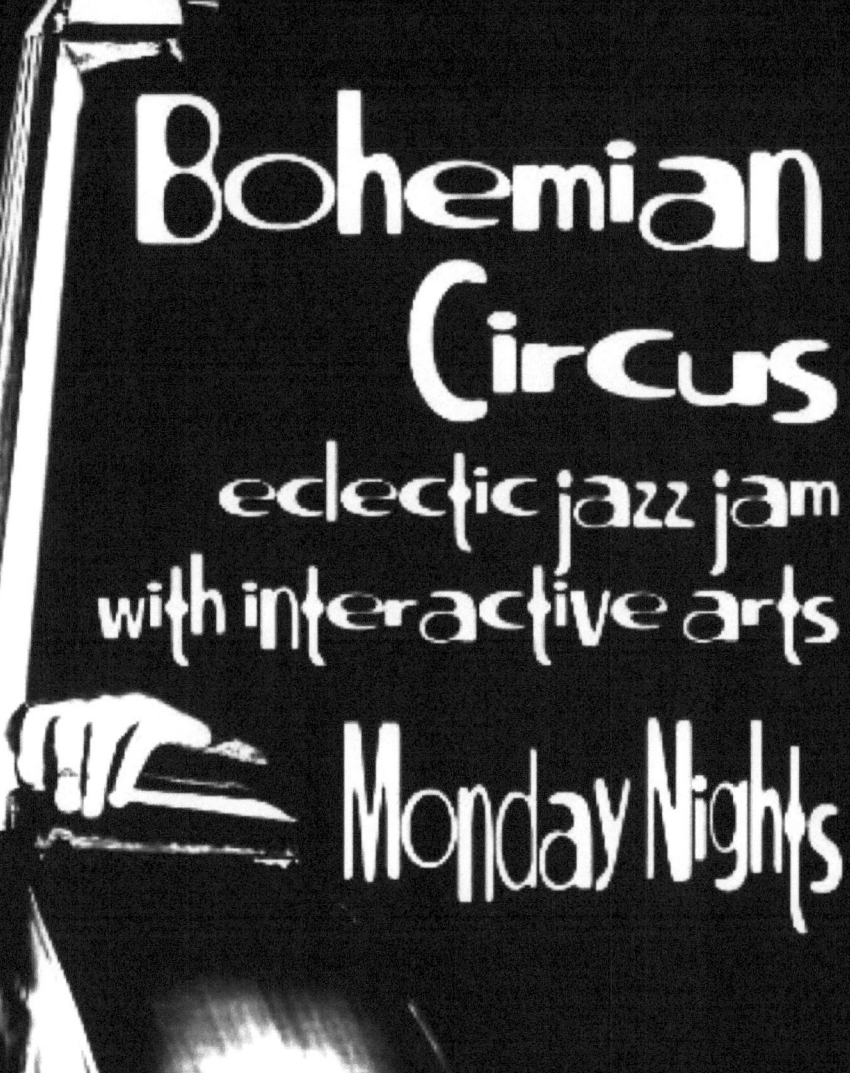

Photography & bio courtesy of Brandon Haynes.

Photog TRIBE

CONCERT

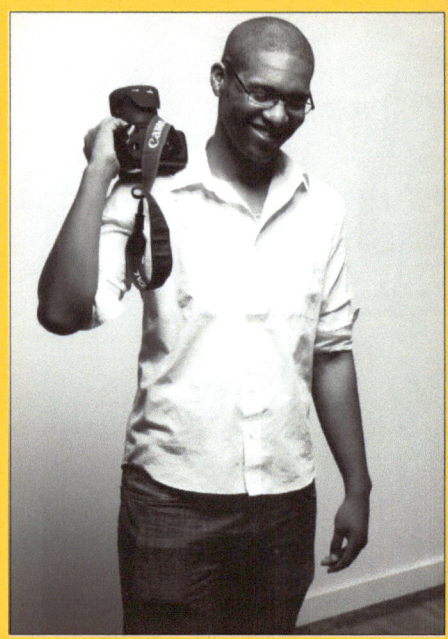

Brandon Haynes is a Brooklyn based photographer and DJ. In 2007, he began to pursue a career in photography. Dark rooms and film processing became his backdrop and he spent endless nights exploring his craft. Brandon started a career in music photography and portraiture which has allowed him to meet and work with some of most talented and unique individuals in the world, including rappers **Mos Def, Talib Kweli** and **Big Daddy Kane.** When he's not shooting, you can find Brandon on the ones and twos in Brooklyn!

To view more photography or for more information, visit bhaynesphoto.com. ■

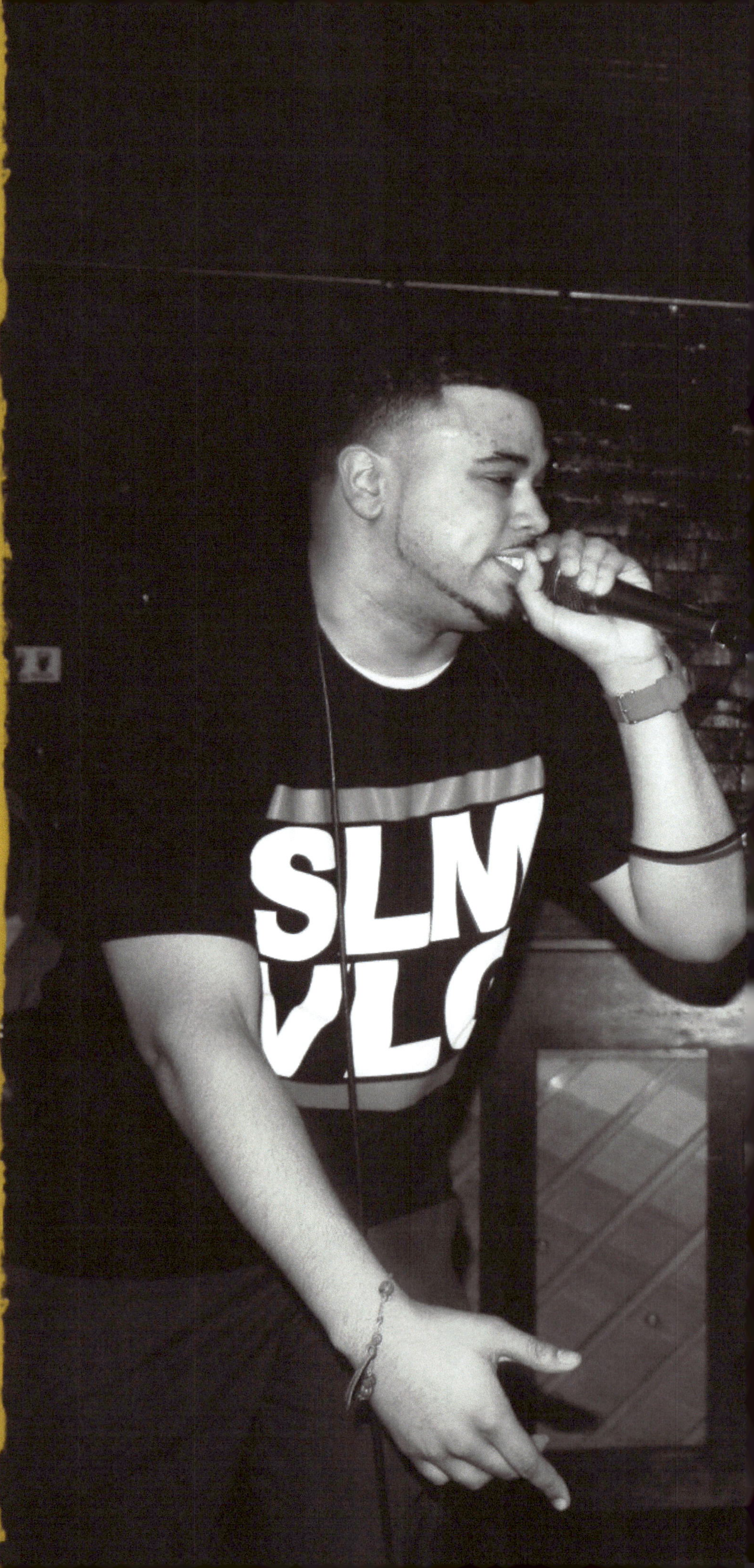

16

CHILDREN OF THE NIGHT

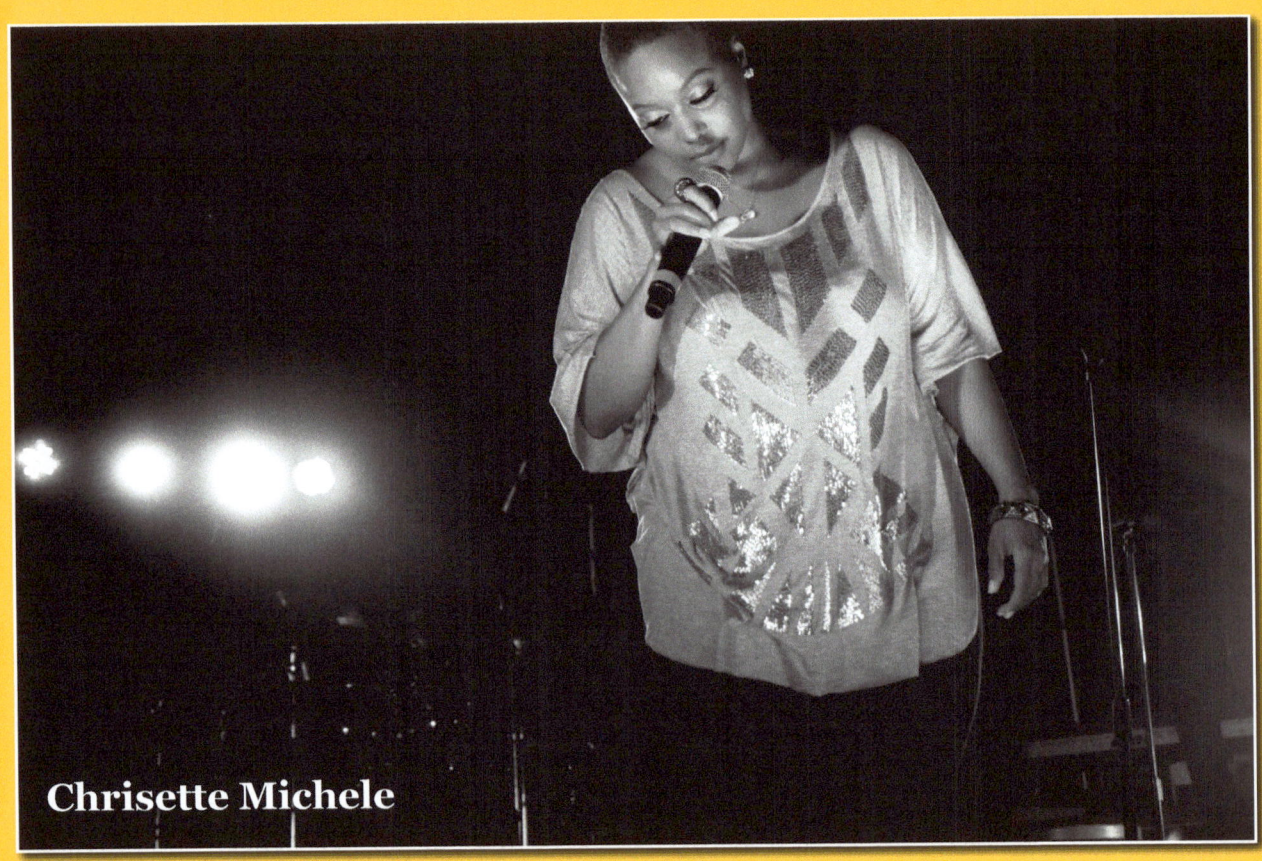

Chrisette Michele

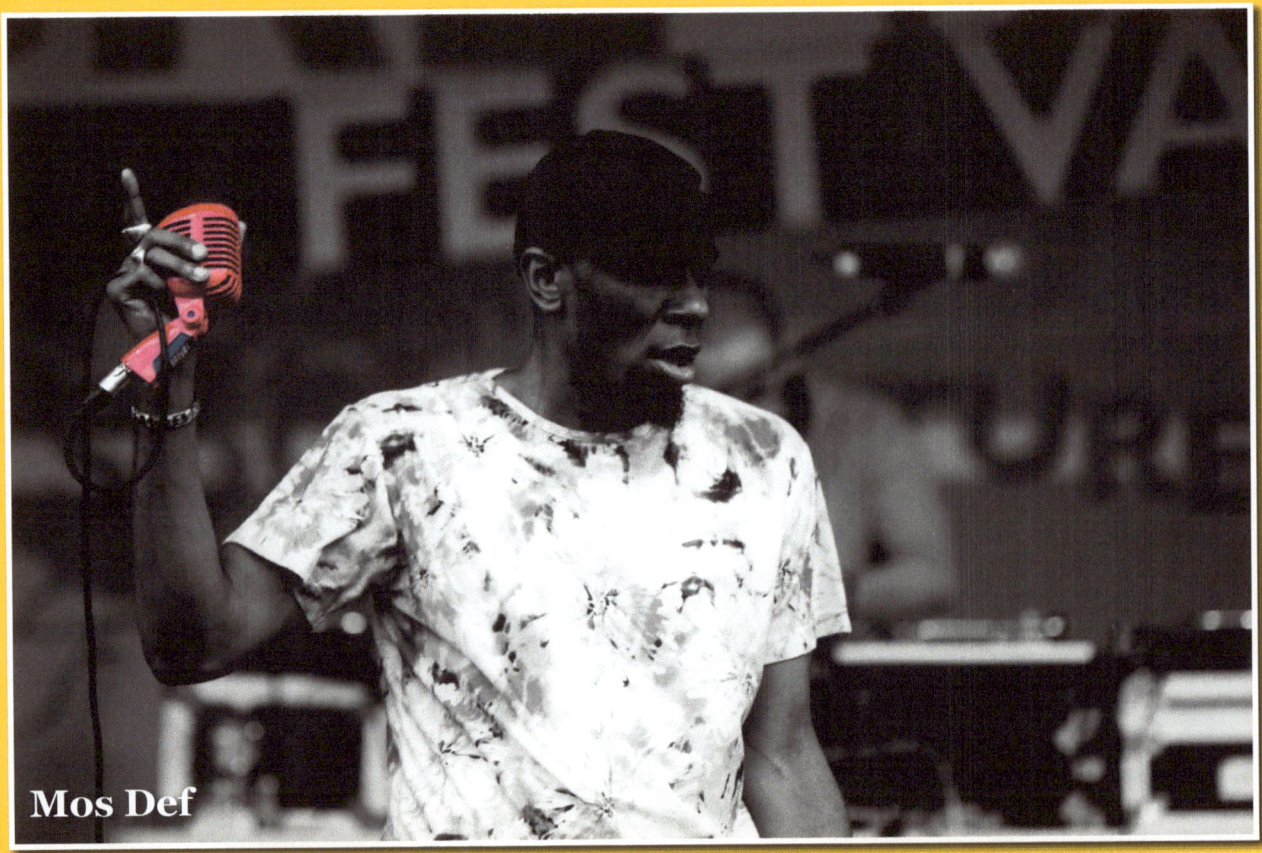

Mos Def

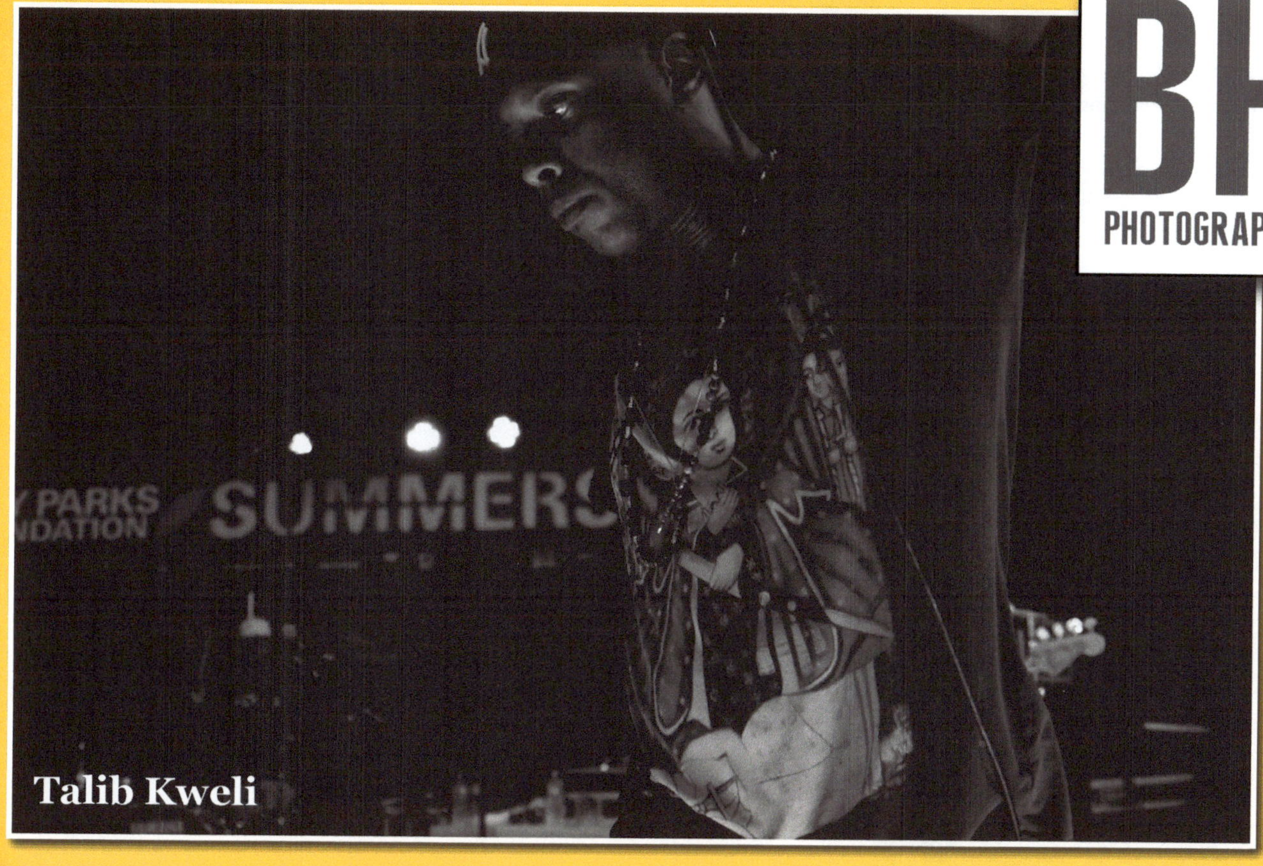

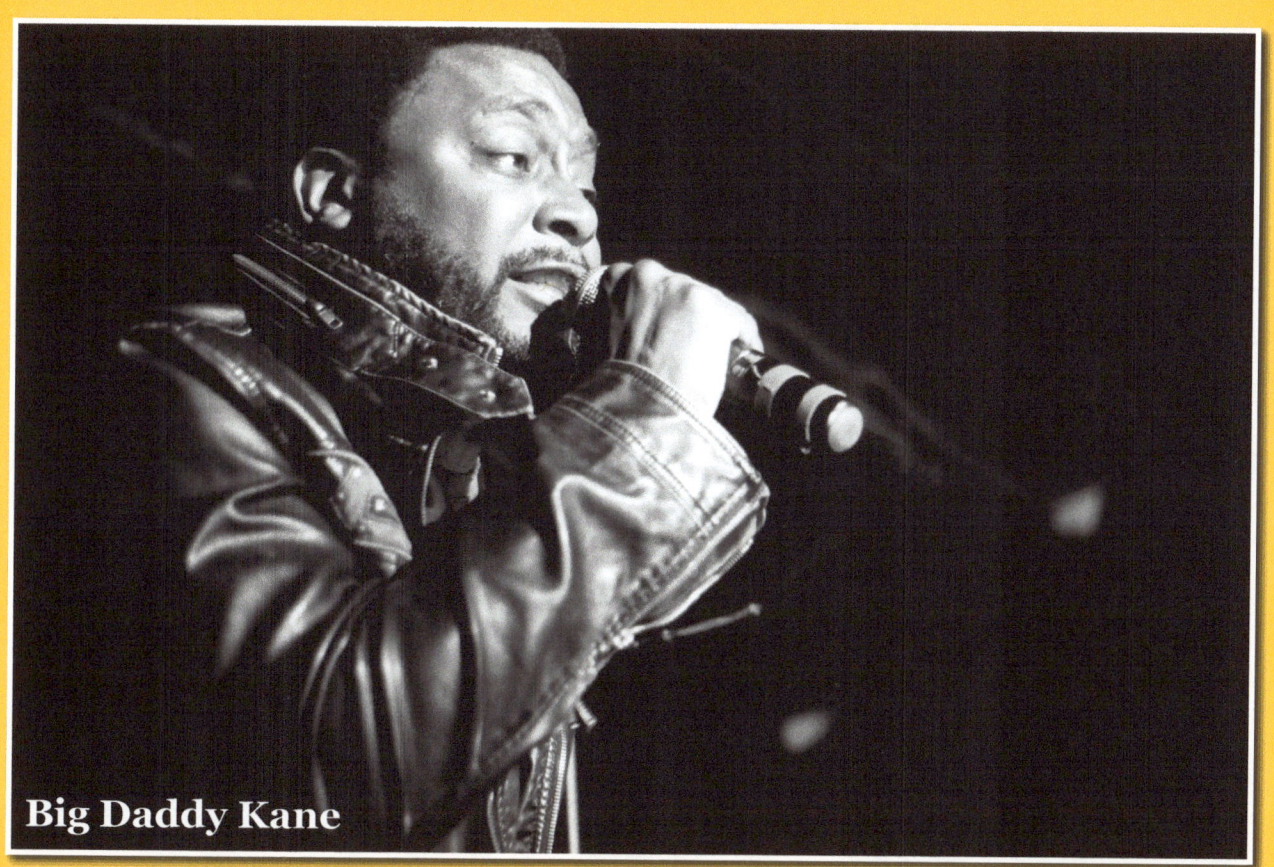

Talib Kweli

Big Daddy Kane

Text by Nichole Martin.
Photograph courtesy of miriammakeba.co.za.

Feature Story

REMEMBERING MAMA AFRICA
Miriam Makeba

Miriam Makeba, South African artist and diva, earned the title of Mama Africa after winning the world over with her harmonic crisp, South Africa-tinged vocals that sung of a country she loved and the injustices suffered there. The voice that gave courage and comfort to South Africans, who rallied against apartheid, became the one of the first African singers to be recognized as a worldwide sensation.

Born Zenzil Miriam Makeba in 1932, in Johannesburg, Makeba began her professional singing career as a featured artist with the South African jazz group the Manhattan Brothers in the 1950's. Shortly thereafter, she formed an all-female group, The Skylarks, and, in 1956, released **'Pata Pata'** which became one her most famous songs. Nevertheless, in spite of her early success, Makeba struggled financially receiving little in payment for her recordings and no provisional royalties.

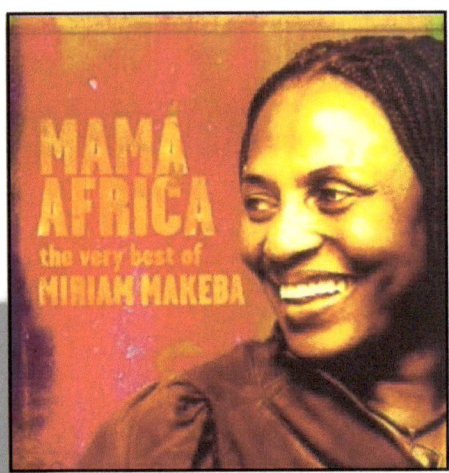

Miriam Makeba

Her big break came in 1959, when a short guest appearance in the anti-apartheid documentary ***Come Back to Africa*** left a lasting impression on the film's producer and director **Lionel Rogosin**. Rogosin would later organize a visa for her to attend the film's premiere in Italy. That same year, Makeba arrived in the United States and debuted on *The Steve Allen Show*.

Upon her return to South Africa later that year to attend her mother's funeral, Makeba was forbidden entry into the country because of her anti-apartheid views. In 1960, she signed with **RCA records** and released her self-titled first studio album, *Miriam Makeba*. Her second studio album, *The World of Miriam Makeba*, followed in 1963, the same year her South African citizenship and right to return to her country was permanently revoked after Makeba testified against apartheid regime before the United Nations.

In 1966, Makeba won a Grammy Award for Best Folk Recording for *An Evening with Belafonte/Makeba*. Offering the world perhaps the first American album to represent Zulu, Sotho and Swahili songs, Makeba continued to color the social and political landscape when, in 1968, her third marriage to civil rights activist and **Black Panther, Stokley Carmichael**, caused further controversy for her in the United States where record deals and tours were subsequently cancelled. The couple expatriated to Guinea for the next 15 years and Makeba was appointed Guinea's official delegate to the United Nations for which she won the **Don Hammarskjold Peace Award** in 1986.

That same year, Makeba joined **Paul Simon** on his wildly successful *Graceland* world tour and was propelled back into spotlight. After touring with Simon, Makeba released *Sangoma* with Warner Bros. Records and the autobiography, *Makeba: My Story*, was published shortly after and translated into German, Dutch, French and Italian. In 1990, upon the fall of apartheid and **Nelson Mandela's** release from a twenty-seven year political imprisonment, Mandela persuaded Makeba to return home to South Africa. Still, she was back in the states the next year recording *Eyes of Tomorrow* with **Dizzy Gillespie**, **Nina Simone** and Hugh Makela- a legendary African artist in his own right and Makeba's second husband.

Over the next 15 years, Miriam Makeba continued to write music and perform though peace and humanitarian activism became her primary mission for which she received countless awards and accolades. In 2005, Makeba began a farewell tour performing to packed halls in each of the countries she had visited throughout her storied career and, on November 9, 2008, after singing her hit song 'Pata Pata' to a vibrant Italian audience, Makeba suffered a heart attack and was unable to be revived. Her music, her legacy of activism, and her voice ready to speak frankly to injustice, lives on. **Visit miriammakeba.co.za** ∎

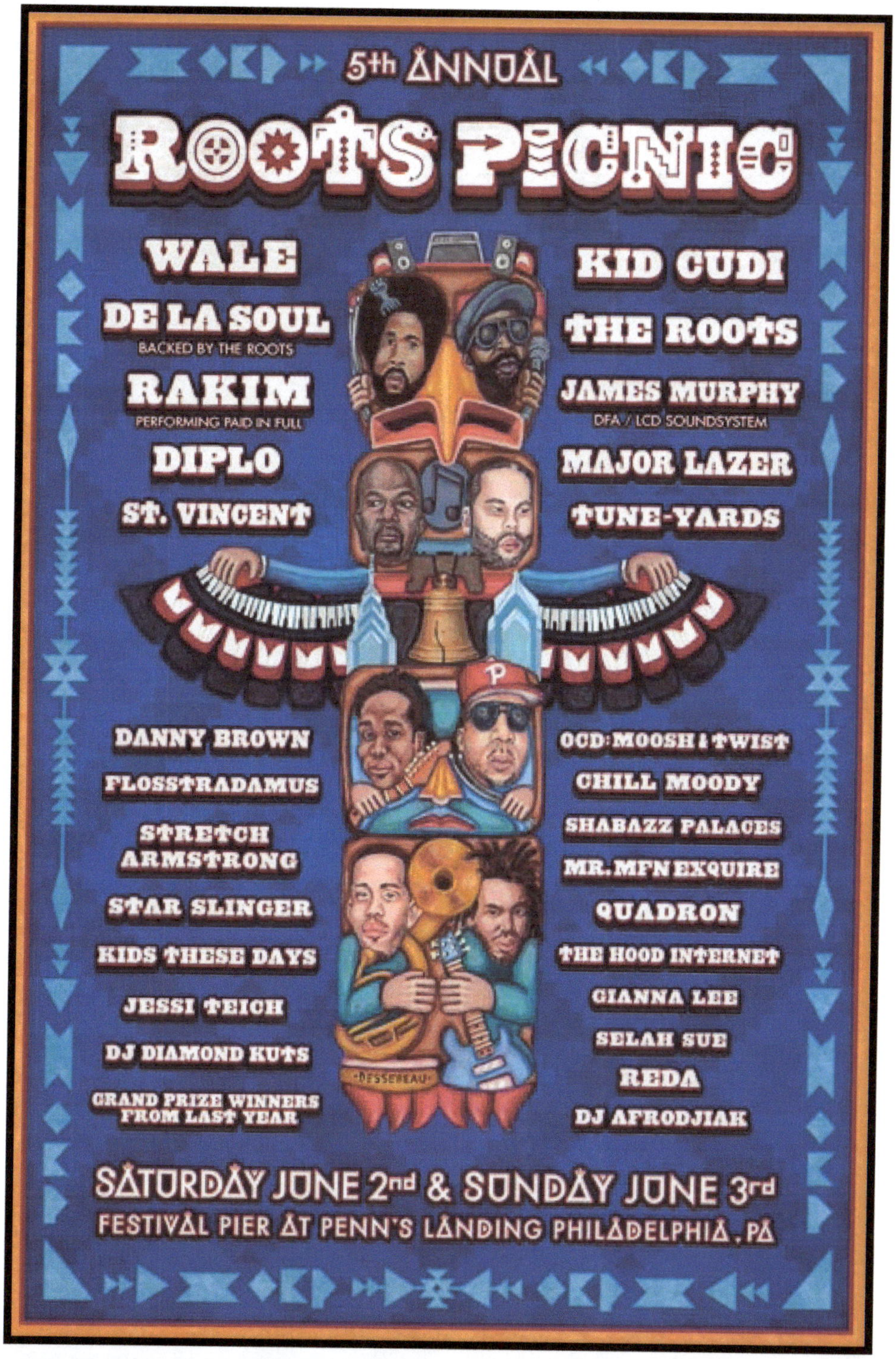

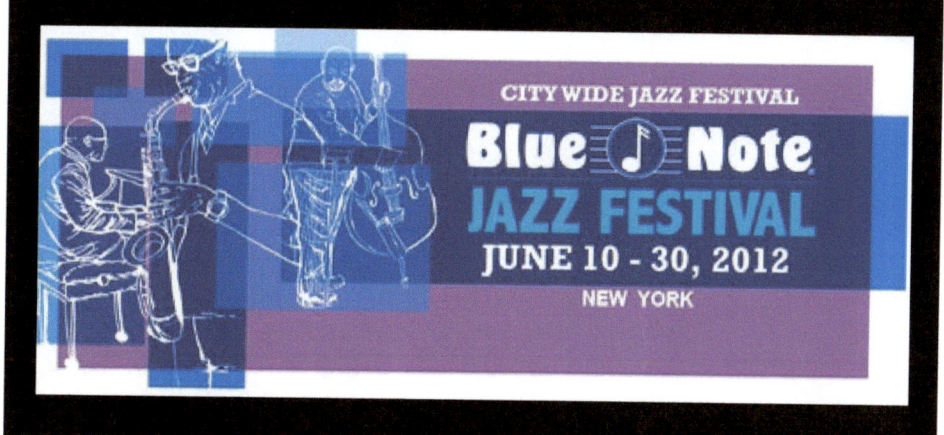

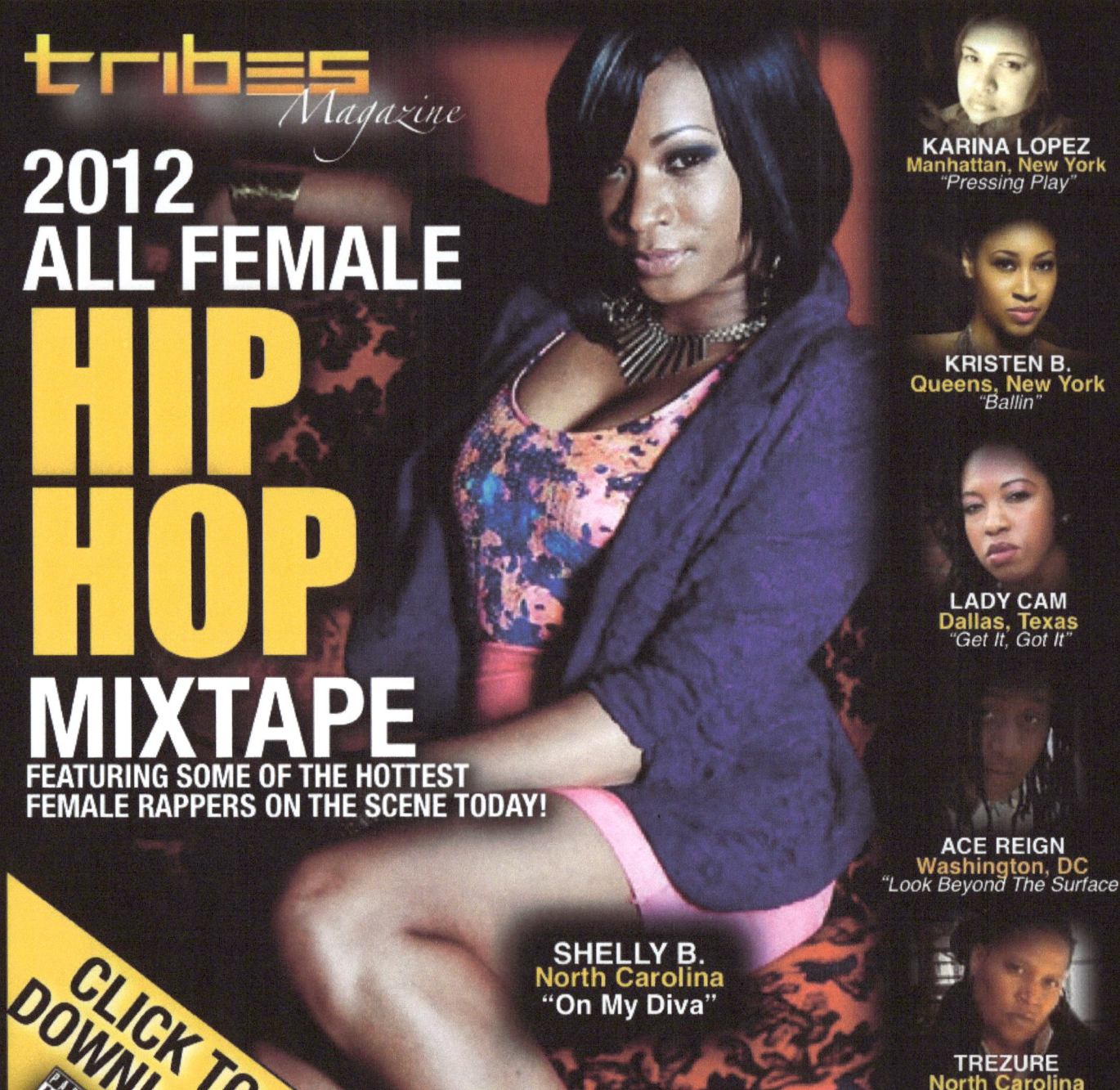

Text by N.M. Solomon, CMIS Staff Writer.
Photograph from Gotye.com.

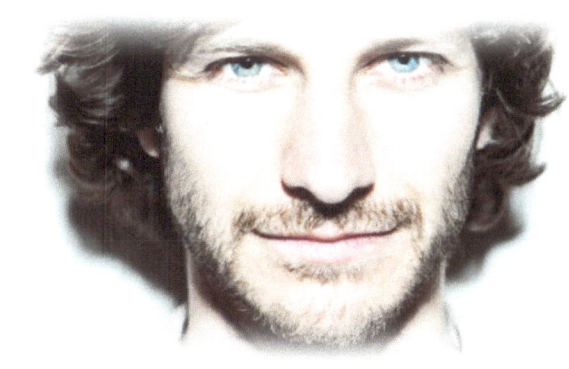

Music TRIBE

Gotye's Indie Domination

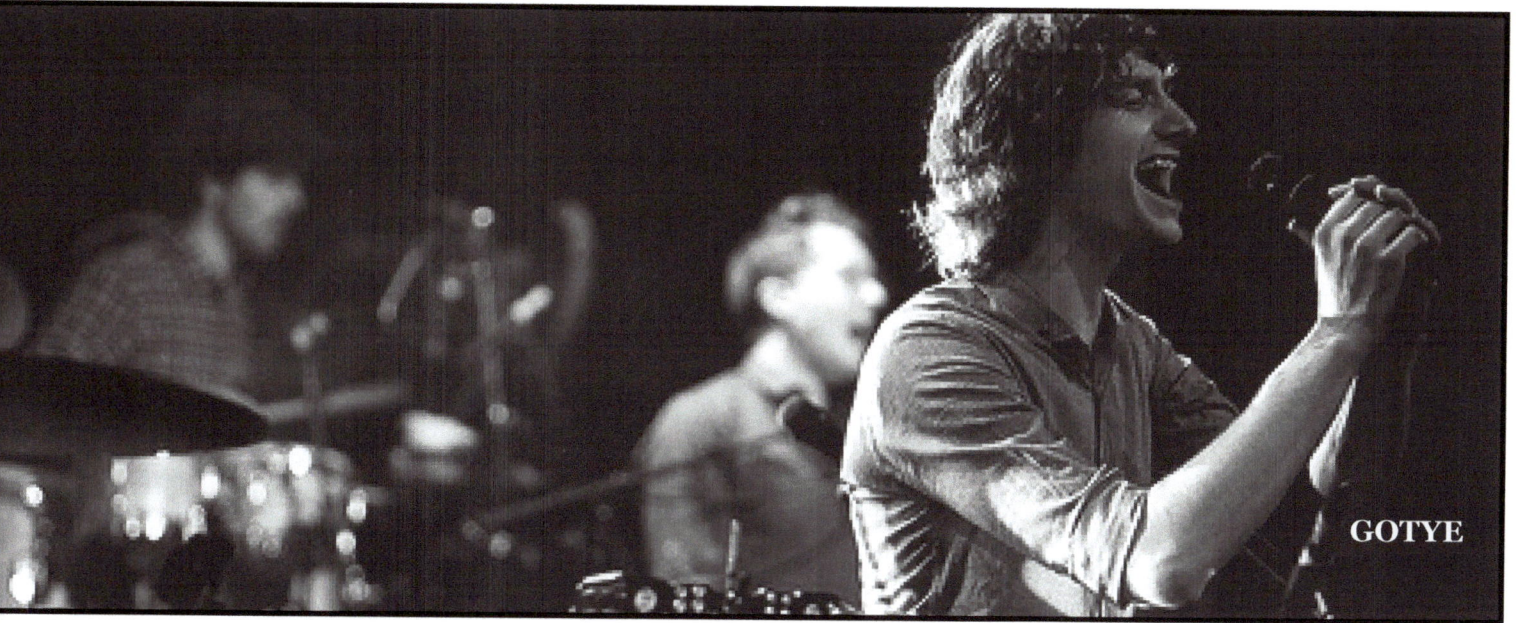

GOTYE

Australian indie singer, songwriter, & producer, Gotye, is dominating nearly every corner of the music charts with his single "Somebody That I Used To Know". In the U.S. alone, the song has remained on **Billboard's Hot 100** for the now fourth consecutive week in a row and digital sales have reached more than 400,000 units in the past three weeks alone.

Upon completion of his second solo album, Like Drawing Blood, Gotye set up a recording studio in a barn on a 13-acre plot of farm. He wanted complete isolation from negative influences and wanted to cultivate his own organic musical creativity sond the soul searching payed off with

"Somebody That I Used" to Know now number one in 13 countries, including the U.S. and U.K.

In fact, Gotye almost didn't finish the smash single and marketing the music proved a challenge for him. "I was disappointed. I couldn't find a release for Canada and the U.S. But because "Somebody That I Used to Know" took off on YouTube...opportunities changed quite rapidly.

"I was quite prepared to put the album out myself and invest a whole heap of money I'd saved over the last couple of years just working with a distributor and doing all the marketing myself."

Released initially in Australia on the independent label Eleven (distributed by Universal), the album quickly

shot to number one and began to spread in other countries. He began outselling Universal's flagship artists including **Jessie J** and **Drake**. In addition, the music video that was supposed to be viral-only became the official video for the single.

Since its upload, "Somebody That I Used to Know" has gained over 153 million views. Now the song appears in several ads, TV shows including **FOX's "Glee"**, and collection of major motion pictures. Strategizing and executing through social media and word of mouth, guerrilla marketing has helped Gotye reach a wide-ranging audience. With a simple YouTube upload, **Facebook & Twitter** posts, the independent road has turned him into a global success. **To listen and learn more, visit gotye.com.** ■

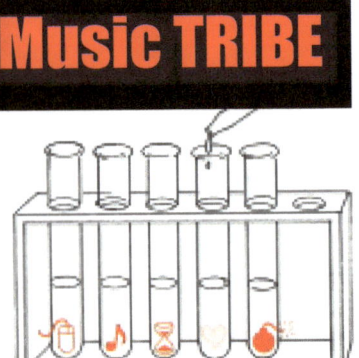

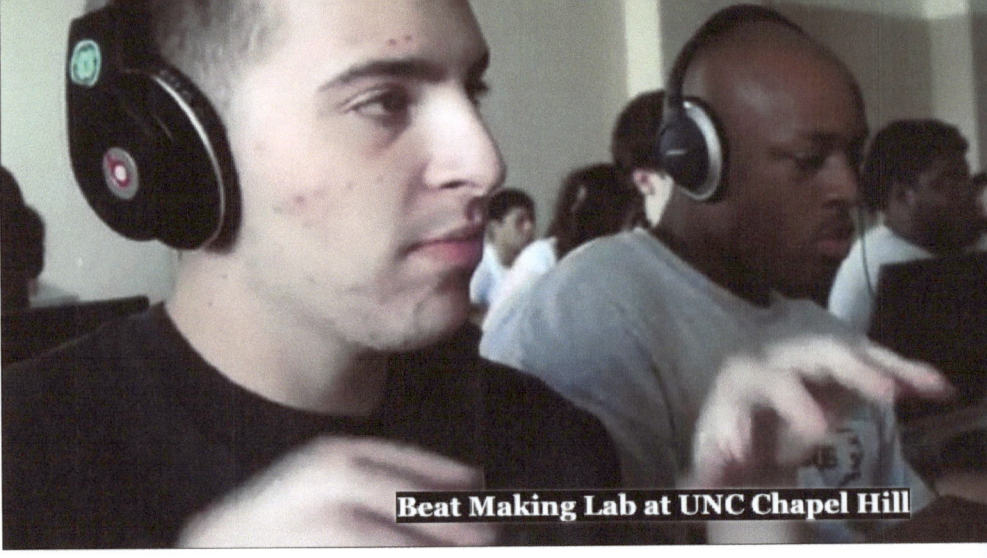

Beat Making Lab at UNC Chapel Hill

TAR HEEL TRACKS

UNC Beat Making Lab Students Sample NC Artists to Raise Money for Congolese Youth

UNC Professor Pierce Freelon and beat battle champion Stephen Levitin co-teach the Beat Making Lab - an innovative course offered in the Music Department at the **University of North Carolina at Chapel Hill**. Co-founded by Levitin and Dr. Mark Katz, the Beat Making Lab teaches sample-based music

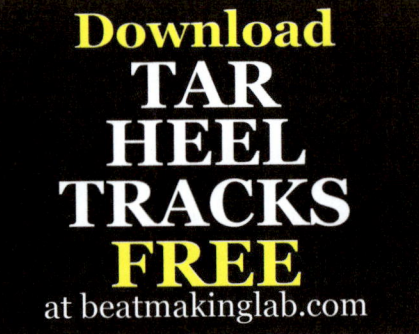

Pierce Freelon and Stephen Levitin

production, history and entrepreneurship to musicians and non-musicians.

On May 13th, **Shuffle Magazine** and **ARTVSM** released the Beat Making Lab's FREE debut album, **Tar Heel Tracks**. The 13-song collection, organized by **Pierce Freelon** and Stephen Levitin, features original Hip Hop, Dance and Electronica, produced by UNC undergraduate students. All production on Tar Heel Tracks samples from other artists based in North Carolina including the **Avett Brothers, Lee Fields, The Foreign Exchange, The Old Ceremony**, and **Nnenna Freelon**. In addition to co-teaching the Beat Making Lab, Pierce Freelon and Levitin are founders of ARTVSM (pronounced Artivism) - a company that merges art and activism by any medium necessary. ARTVSM will bring the Beat Making Lab curriculum to 16 **Congolese youth** in Goma this summer through Yole! Africa.

Download TAR HEEL TRACKS FREE at beatmakinglab.com

Founded in 2000 by Congolese filmmaker **Petna Ndaliko** and Dutch anthropologist **Ellen Lammers**, with a mission to "promote peace through art and culture," Yole is a vibrant center for artistic creation and cultural exchange. Freelon and Levitin will travel to the center in the Congo this July to set up a fully functioning beat making Lab in Goma. They have successfully raised $5,000 through an Indiegogo crowd-funding campaign to help pay for a laptop, headphones, speakers, beat making software and travel.

For more information, visit beatmakinglab.com.

Contact Pierce Freelon at artvsm@gmail.com. ■

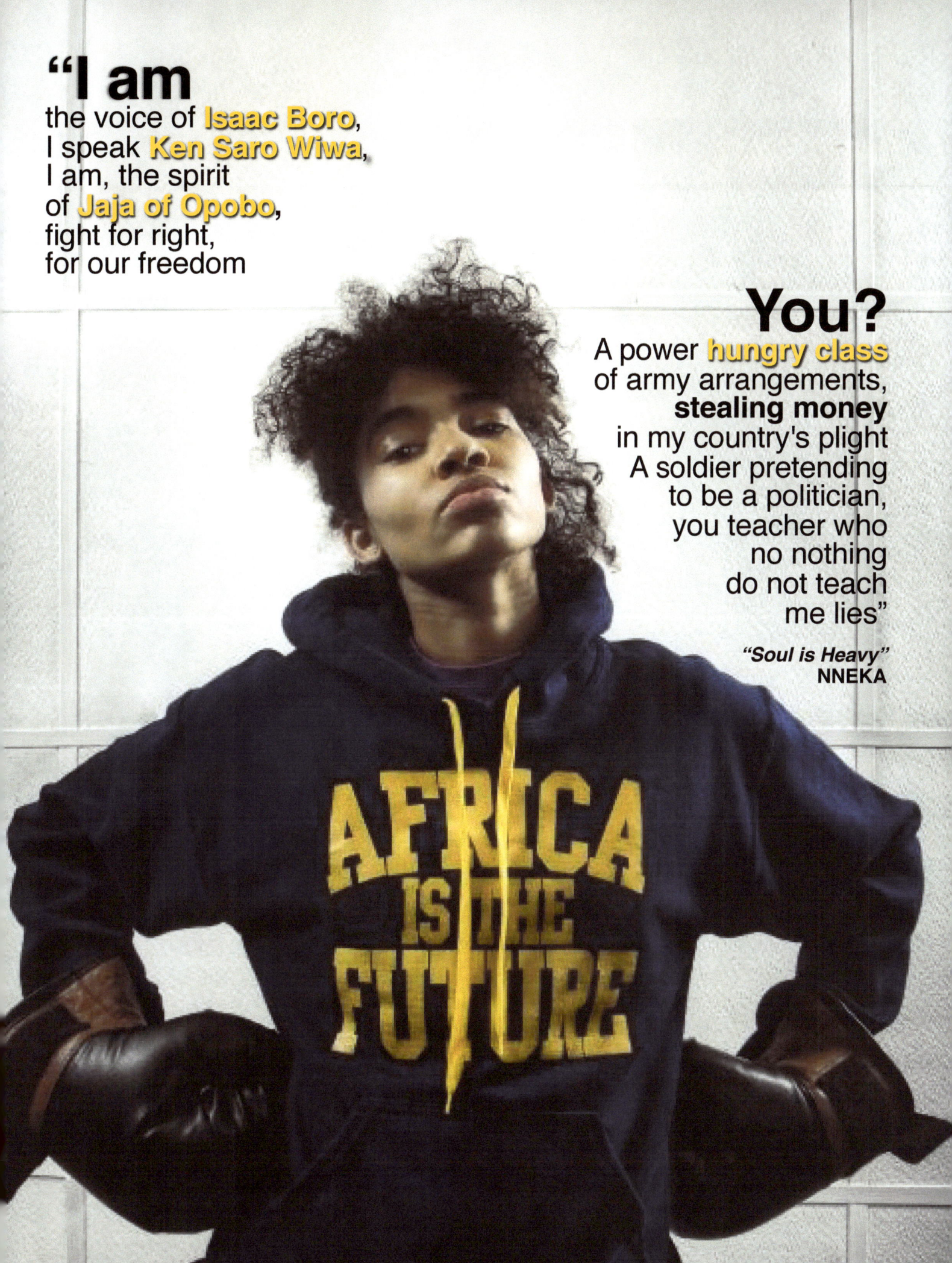

"I am
the voice of Isaac Boro,
I speak Ken Saro Wiwa,
I am, the spirit
of Jaja of Opobo,
fight for right,
for our freedom

You?
A power hungry class
of army arrangements,
stealing money
in my country's plight
A soldier pretending
to be a politician,
you teacher who
no nothing
do not teach
me lies"

"Soul is Heavy"
NNEKA

AFRICA IS THE FUTURE

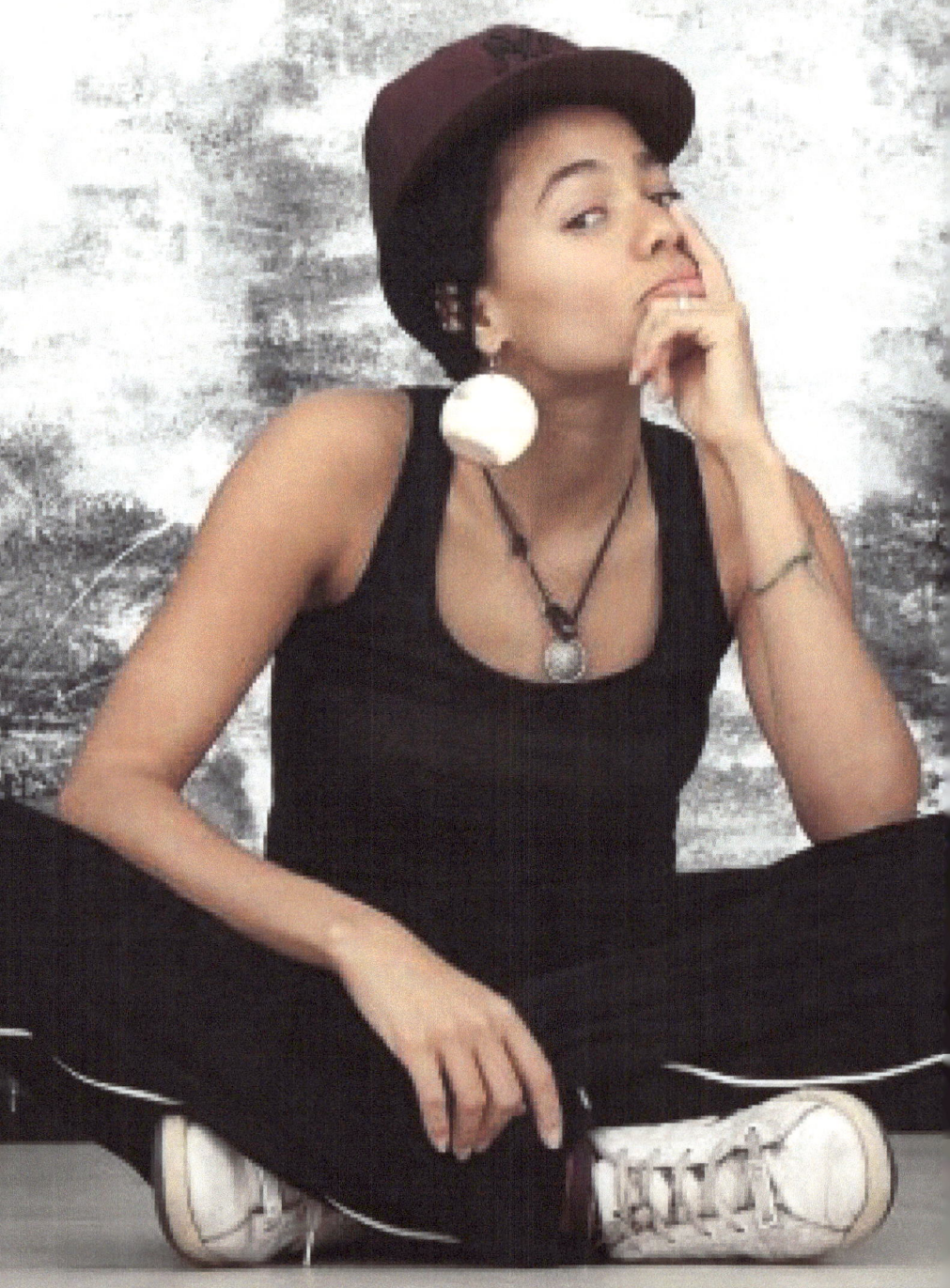

NNEKA

Text by Leslie Cunningham.
Photographs courtesy of Nnekaworld.com.

SOUL IS HEAVY

Interview with Nigerian Songbird, Nneka Egbuna

A talented and passionate singer/songwriter and rapper, Nneka has caught the attention of *TRIBES Magazine* before.

Appearing on the ***TRIBES Magazine's Top 24 Independent Artist Tracks on Myspace*** in 2008, Nneka, even some four years ago was making a name for herself and contemporary Nigeria musical culture and politics in Nigeria and around Europe, with her soulful acoustic-heavy ballads and freestyle raps on capitalism, poverty and war. Nneka remained on **TRIBES Top 24** for several months that year followed by a review in our Music Tribe. Now, Nneka is back in an eagerly **anticipated interview with *TRIBES Magazine*,** to speak to the family about her musical journey from Warri to Hamburg, Africa and Europe to the U.S, and the mission she pursues through her art in this moment of global connectivity on a platform ready for voices of change and yearning for **The Motherland**.

Described by some as a new-millennium Bob Marley, Nneka Egbuna (meaning 'mother is supreme') first introduced the world to her potent brand of conscious Hip Hop in 2005. The daughter of a Nigerian father and German mother, Nneka was born and raised in Warri, a major oil city in the **Niger Delta** region of Nigeria that has and continues to suffer great political and social upheaval as its citizens and the world vie for access to the regions wealth of natural resources.

At age 19, Nneka swapped work in her stepmother's restaurant in Warri for study abroad, at the University of Hamburg. In a new city, music became a means not only to finance her studies but also a means of survival as Nneka searched for her voice in a radically different cultural community. With Nigeria ever heavy on her mind, Nneka began to use music as her stage to express her love, pain and hopes for her homeland.

Nneka's U.S. album debut, Concrete Jungle, revealed a beautiful, outspoken songbird whose message was delivered in mystical lyrics and passionate sounds with as much depth of feeling and intent as that of any other artist to hit the world stage in recent memory.

Nneka's U.S. album debut, *Concrete Jungle*, revealed a beautiful, outspoken songbird whose message was delivered in mystical lyrics and passionate sounds with as much depth of feeling and intent as that

27

of any other artist to hit the world stage in recent memory. With vocal talent that generates frequent comparisons to legends like **Lauryn Hill, Nina Simone** and **Erykah Badu**, Nneka's unique blend of afrobeat, reggae, pop, and Hip Hop puts her in a class that is currently all her own. Touring stages from Atlanta to Paris, Nneka has opened for **Lenny Kravitz, The Roots, Femi Kuti, Gnarls Barkely** and **Sean Paul** among others and on Nneka's latest album, *Soul Is Heavy*, released September 2011 and still making a splash around the globe, fans will once again be moved by a "raw and honest window into her beliefs on love, pain, politics and God" (nnekaworld.com).

TRIBES: How were you introduced to Hip Hop?

NNEKA: I was introduced to Hip Hop in Warri by a friend of mine who used to work in an okrika shop. These are old second hand clothes that are sent from Europe to Africa. He used to sell these clothes. Well, anyway, I used to work in a small food shop close by. So, in his lunch break time, he used to show me some music on his old walkman. It was Hip Hop.

TRIBES: Can you tell us, how did you get started?

NNEKA: I never really thought I would become a musician. I always loved music, but it was sacred, something I hardly shared with anyone. I have never been a person who would show off with my voice. I was shy and did my thing in a shy way. It was in Germany where I finally began to gain more courage to express myself. Being far way

from Nigeria caused me to do music more than ever. And, so it evolved. I wrote my thoughts and my pain down and all I saw. I met other people, including DJ FarHot from Afghanistan who is still today the main person I work with. We vibed from the beginning. He was searching for his identity within the music and I was eager to express myself. So, we became a team.

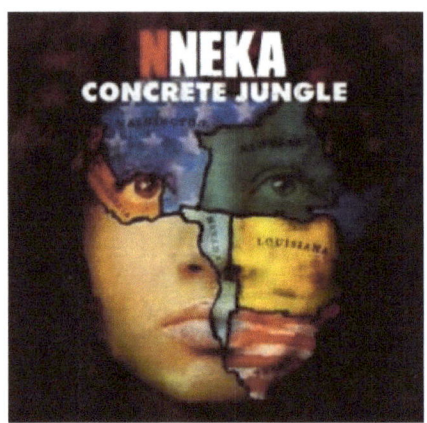

I found a record company that was interested in me, YoMama Records. I played a couple of shows and invited them to see me and two months later, they offered me a record deal. YoMama was then sold to Sony. (That is how I became an artist on a major record company).

TRIBES: You worked with American artists like NAS and The Roots. What is your take on the U.S. Hip Hop scene?

NNEKA: I love conscious music. Hip Hop. Real music. Music with depth and truth. Hip Hop is changing, just like the world. There is good. There is bad. I guess for the good to be identified, there has to be the bad. So they are both necessary.

TRIBES: Why did you dedicate your American album debut, *Concrete Jungle*, to the people of Warri?

NNEKA: *Concrete Jungle* says everything. It is me, my heritage, and an album that speaks for many in pain and plight. The major issue is the Niger Delta, which carved me into who I have become today. Out of anger, you do things either positive or negative. I choose positivity though the source of inspiration is very dark.

TRIBES: You've been compared to Nina Simone, Erykah Badu & Bob Marley. You've sited Fela Kuti, Mos Def and Talib Kweli as some of your influences. Are there any other artists that have influenced your music? Are there other peers making music that excites and inspires you?

NNEKA: I love Keziah Jones. I am a fan of the White Stripes, Victore Uwaifor, King Sunny Ade, Sunny Okosun, Portis Head and more.

TRIBES: We love your "Africa is the Future" sweatshirt on Facebook. In your opinion, is Africa becoming a major player in the international music scene?

NNEKA: Africa is more recognized. It is a good thing. The Nigerian music scene has always been quite vibrant domestically. However, people like the legendary Fela Kuti helped in putting more international focus on African music. Within the last five years the music scene has exploded with new young artists. It is common for artists here to negotiate lucrative endorsements deals within the corporate sector and collaboration with international artists is also becoming a trend. There is a widespread

SOUL IS HEAVY

Naija
in the loud and rowdy
of my world,
there is a secret place
where I find myself.
Can I find you?
Biafra,
the noise of horns
of thirsty Nigerians,
of hustlers, of mothers
confront me as I walk past
Lagos, in prayer
contemplation
like a ghost;
I feel the sorrow of a many.
Still I do not know
how much pain it takes.
Naija,
I walk the island.
I walk the mainland.
I see diversity.
I smell capacity
but still we suffer!
Why?

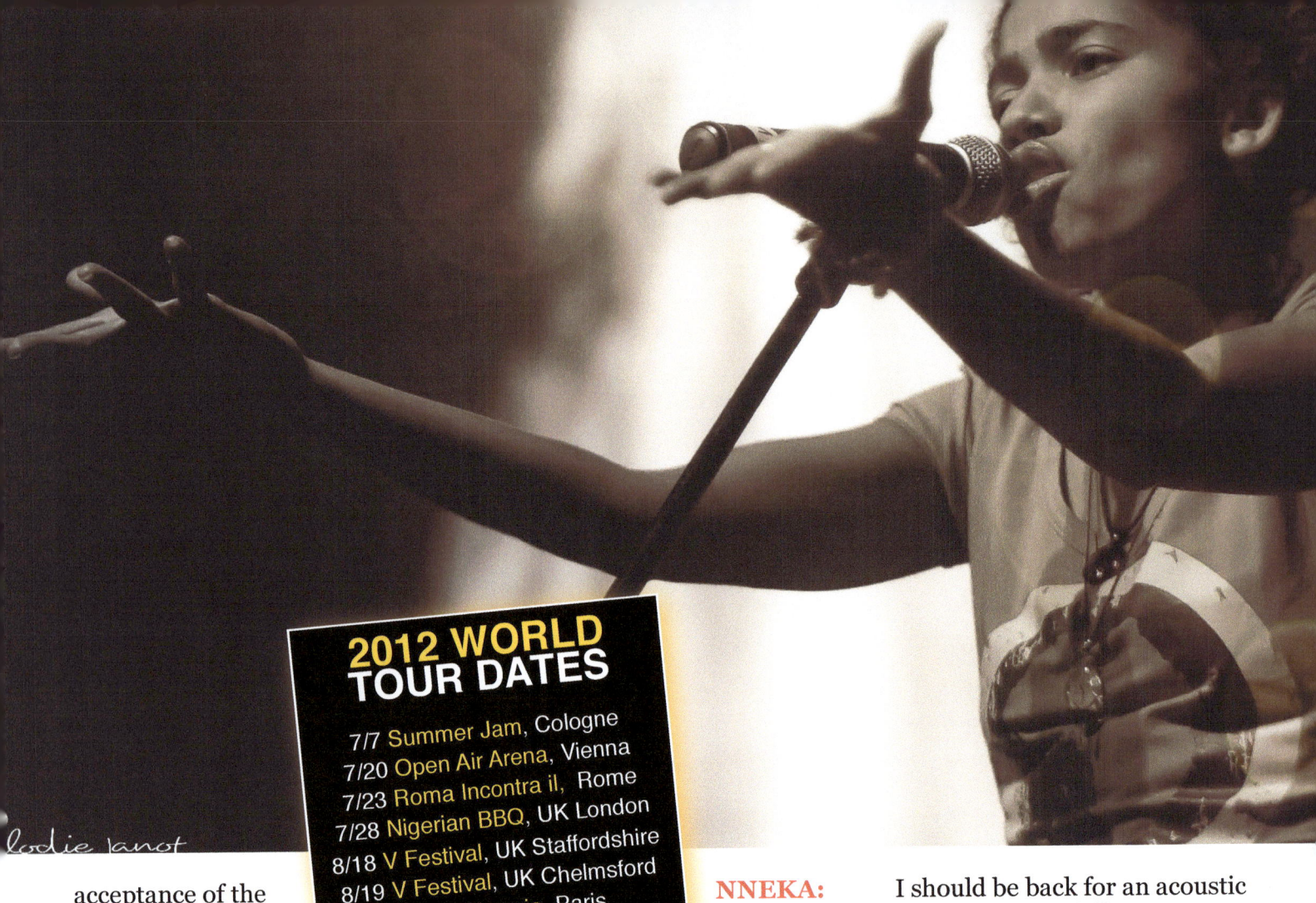

loodie ianot

2012 WORLD TOUR DATES

7/7 Summer Jam, Cologne
7/20 Open Air Arena, Vienna
7/23 Roma Incontra il, Rome
7/28 Nigerian BBQ, UK London
8/18 V Festival, UK Staffordshire
8/19 V Festival, UK Chelmsford
10/12 Olympia, Paris

GET MORE TOUR DATES ON NNEKAWORLD.COM!

acceptance of the music and if you got to nightclubs or bars [in Nigeria], you hardly here any foreign music. Which shows a shift and trend towards what we listen to growing up.

TRIBES: What was it like studying anthropology while creating culture yourself?

NNEKA: It inspired me a lot. University...learning cultures, habits and traditions; and it complimented my musical journey.

TRIBES: Your music shows such commitment to the political plight of your compatriots in the Niger Delta. If you could see one change in the political reality of Nigeria, what would it be?

NNEKA: The way we speak to one another and our corrupt leaders.

TRIBES: Do you consider yourself an independent musician?

NNEKA: Yes, but I am open and willing to listen to peoples opinions.

TRIBES: Are you enjoying the road now that you're achieving U.S. notoriety? Are you enjoying bringing your music to this side of the Atlantic?

NNEKA: Yes. I have been touring and I am glad to spread this message of love across the globe. The U.S. has been very receptive and the last tour was very successful.

I should be back for an acoustic set. Something different.

TRIBES: Who are some other great Nigerian artists we should know about that are making great music and speaking truth to power?

NNEKA: Babatunde, Ade Bantu, Keziah Jones, Asa, Seun Kuti, Femi Kuti, Wura Samba, Oranmiyan and More.

TRIBES: Thank you for sharing your journey with *TRIBES Magazine*.

NNEKA: Thank you. **Love and Light.**

To listen and learn more, visit nnekaworld.com. ■

CONCERTS FOR THE PEOPLE

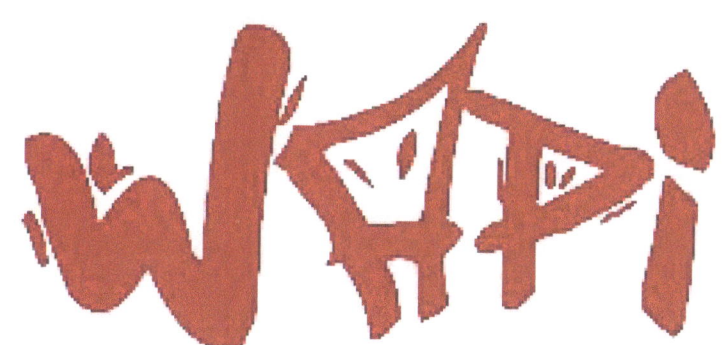

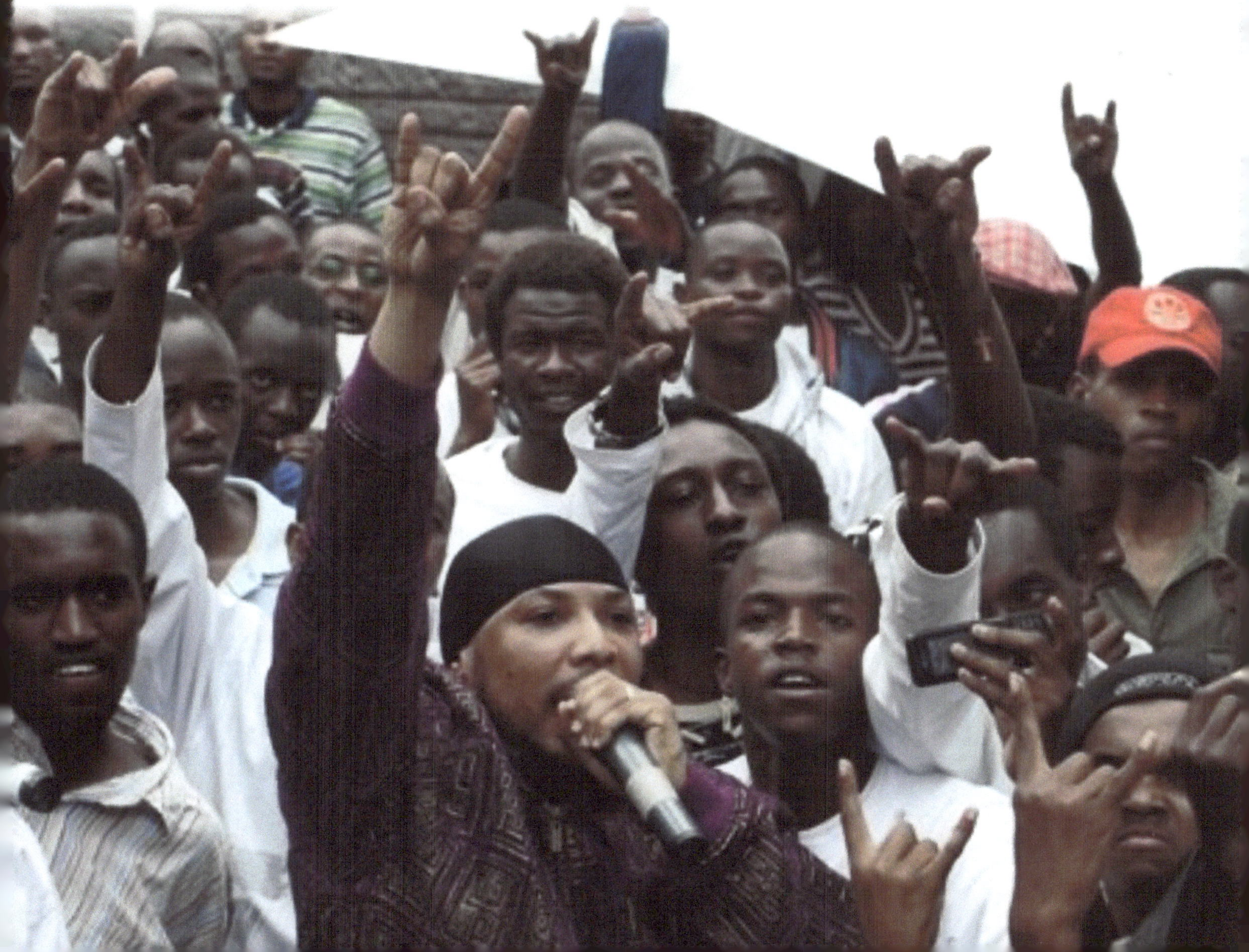

WAPI

(Words and Pictures) is an arts platform for urban youth in **Nairobi, Kenya**. It is governed by the **British Council** and is the established platform for young creative people in Kenya to showcase their artistic, musical and poetic talent and to win peer recognition. **Photos compliments of Wapi Kenya.**

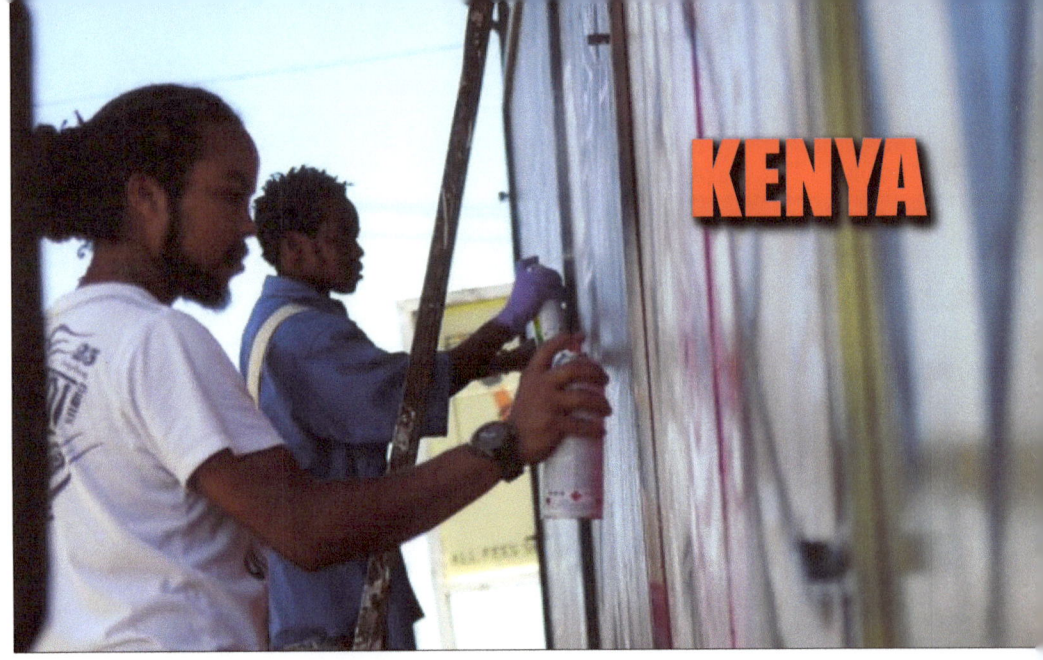

KENYA

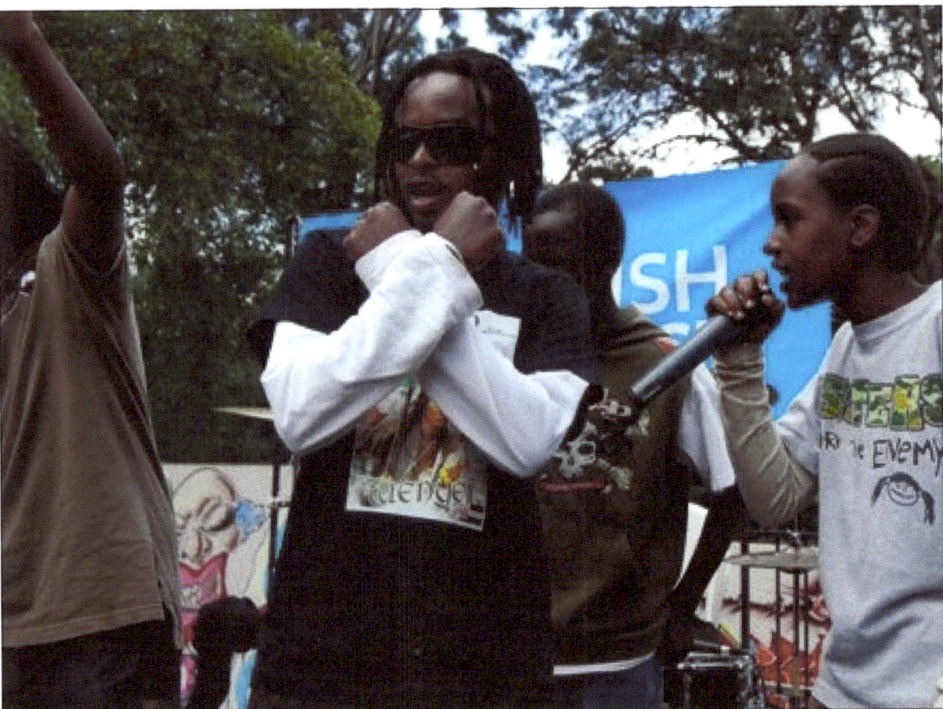

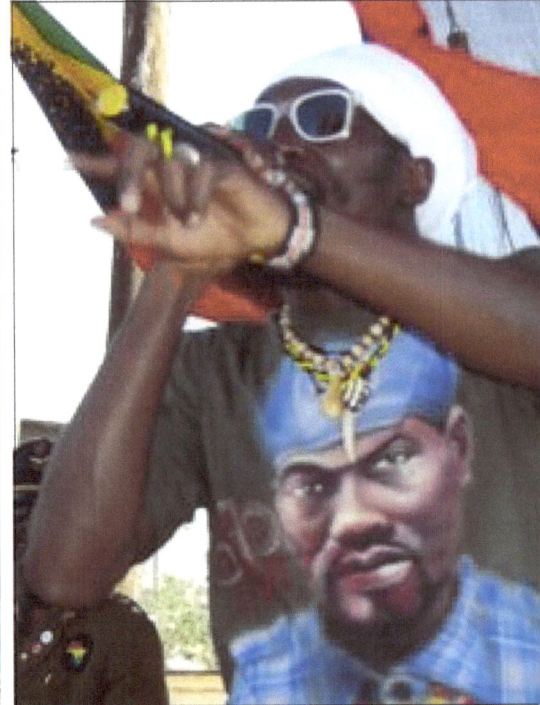

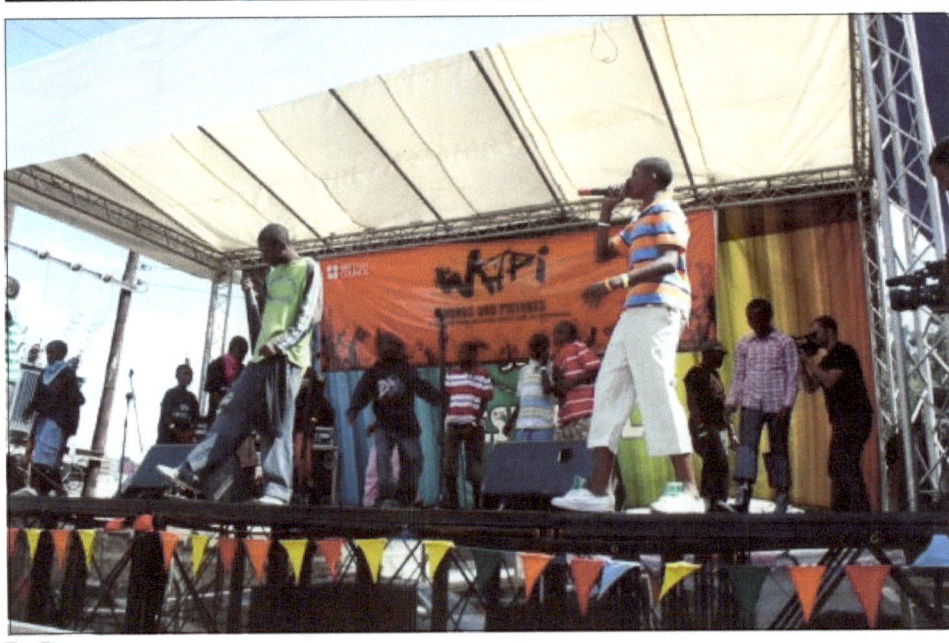

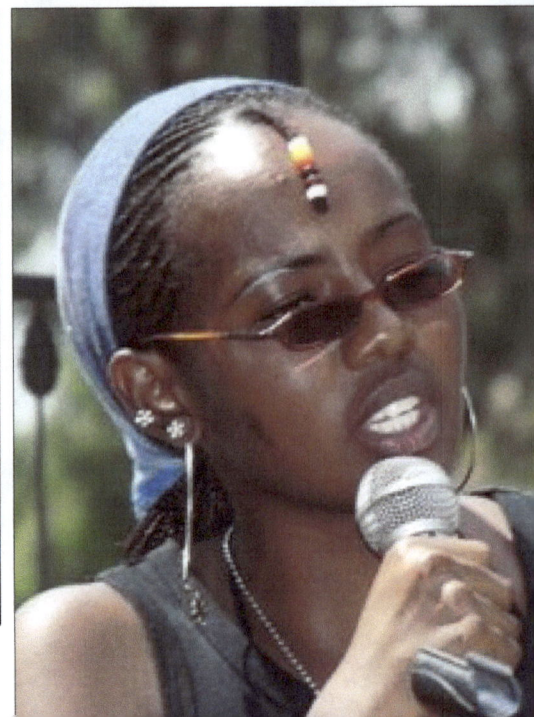

32

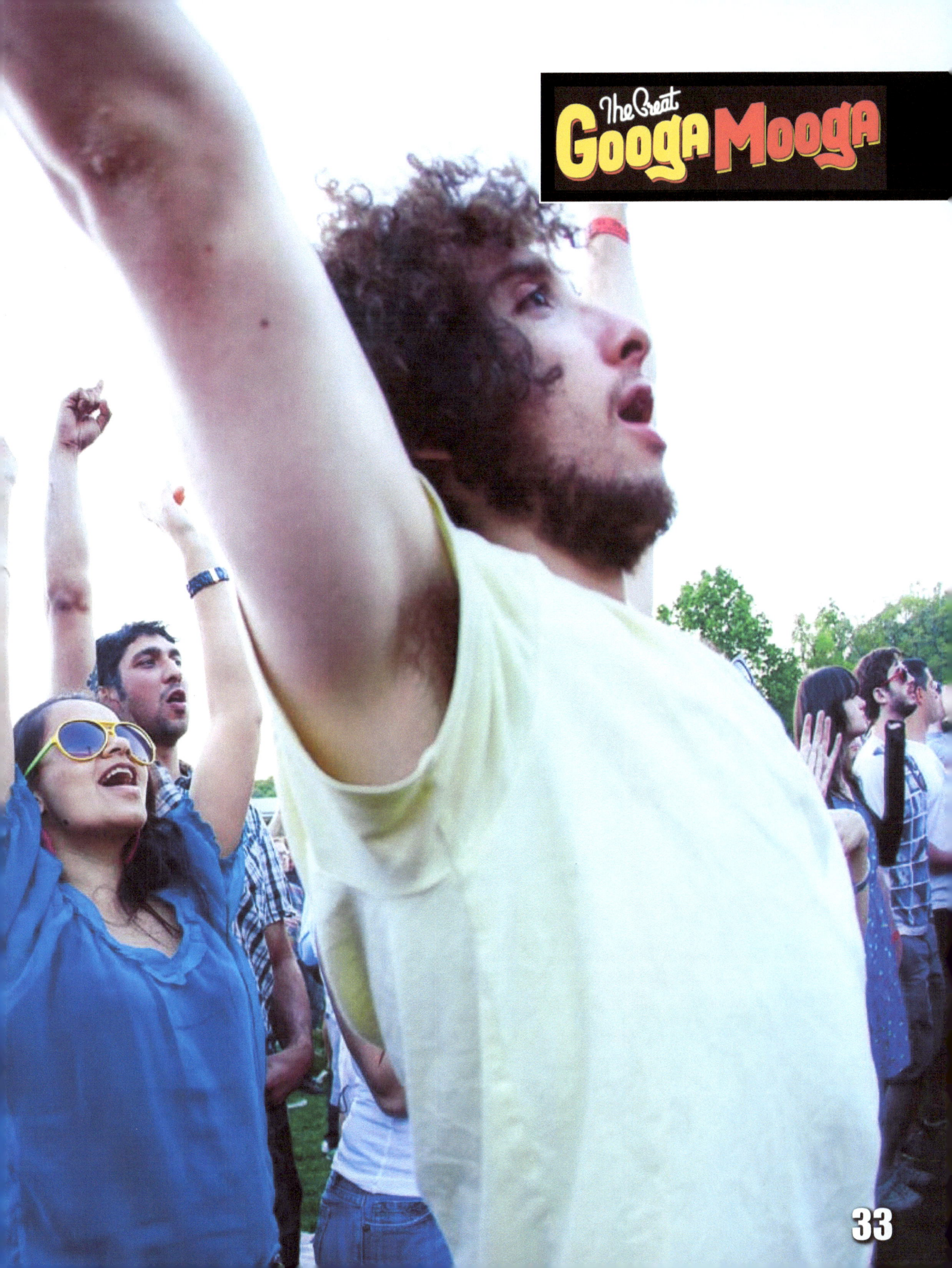

Great Googa Mooga

is held annually in Broolyn's historic Prospect Park and is a celebration of life's greatest pleasures: gathering with friends and neighbors to eat, drink, talk, laugh, dance, linger and just be together. Native New Yorker Becky Yee captured the May 2012 event featuring *The Roots*. **Visit BeckyYee.com.** ■

BROOKLYN

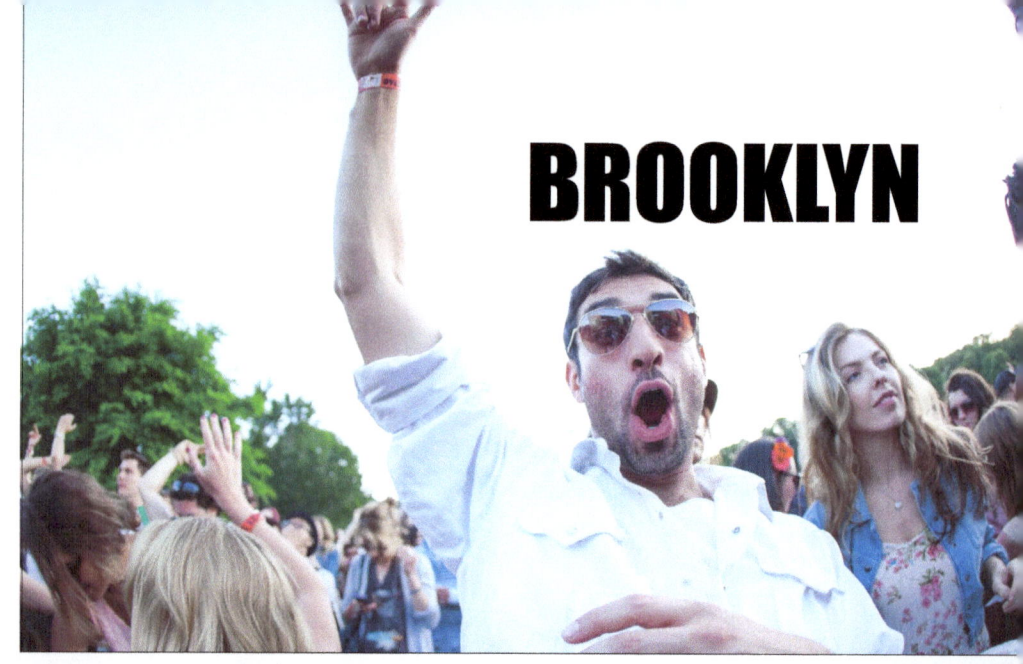

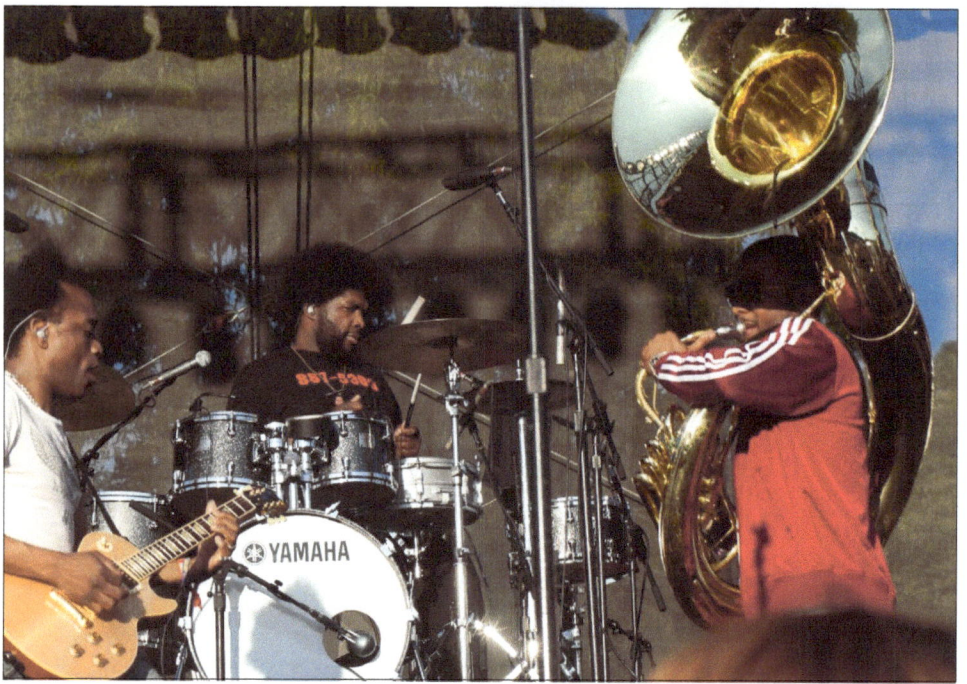

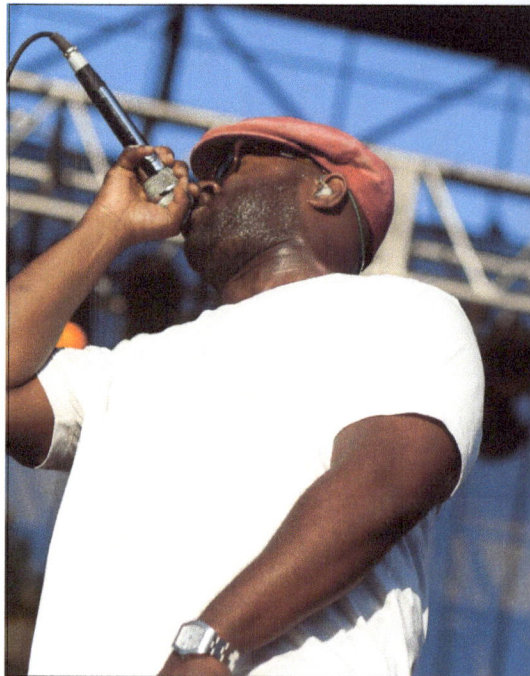

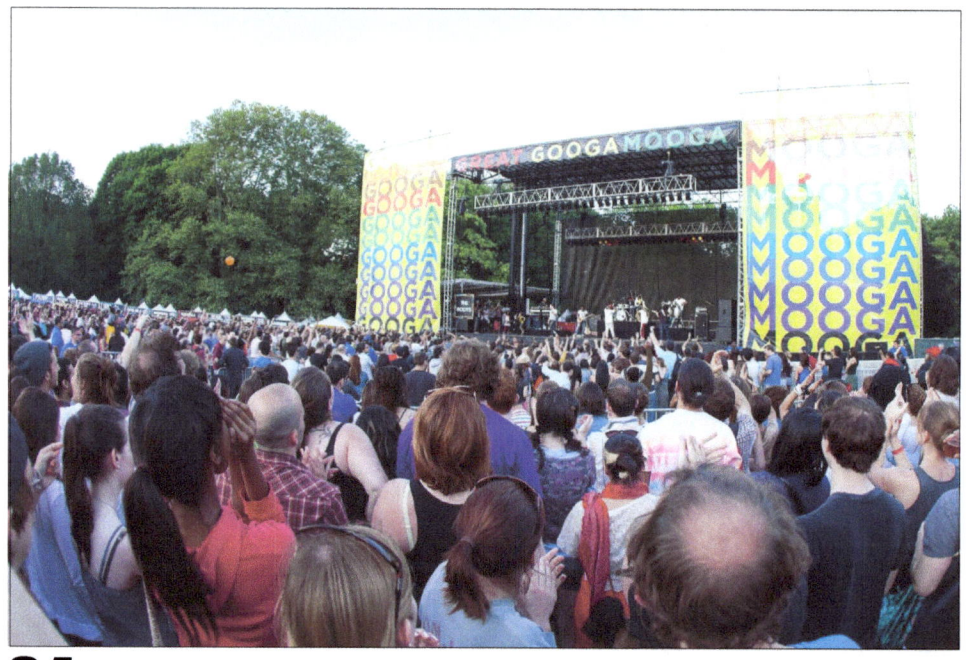

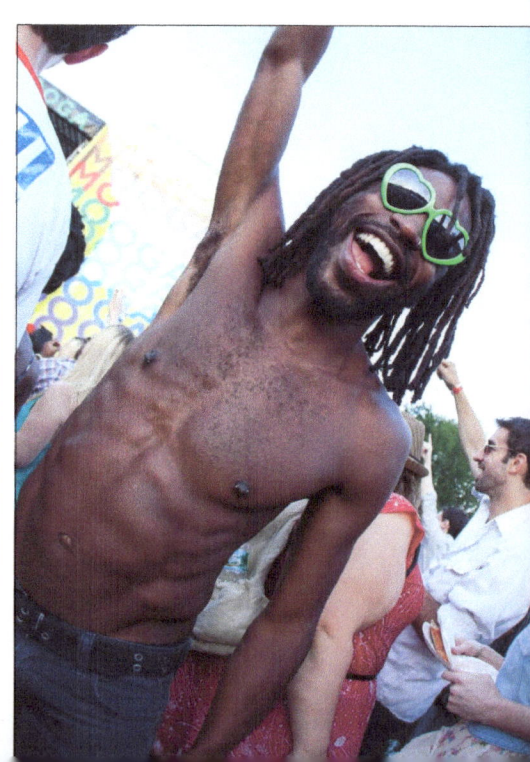

TRIBES' TOP TEN
WORLD SUMMER
CONCERT
PICKS FOR 2012

★**Roots Picnic**, Philadelphia, PA - June 2-3
★**Blue Note Jazz Festival,** Brooklyn, NY - June 10-30
★**Fly Poet Summer Classic**, Hollywood, California - July 7
★**Wireless Festival**, London, UK- July 6-8
★**Underground Music Showcase**, Denver, Co - July 19
★**Ottawa Bluesfest,** Ontario, CAN- July 4-15
★**Slightly Stupid Tour**, Raleigh, NC - July 25
★**V Festival,** Chelmsford, London - August 19
★**Made in American Music Festival**, Philadelphia, PA - September 1
★**A3C Hip Hop Festival**, Atlanta, GA- October 4

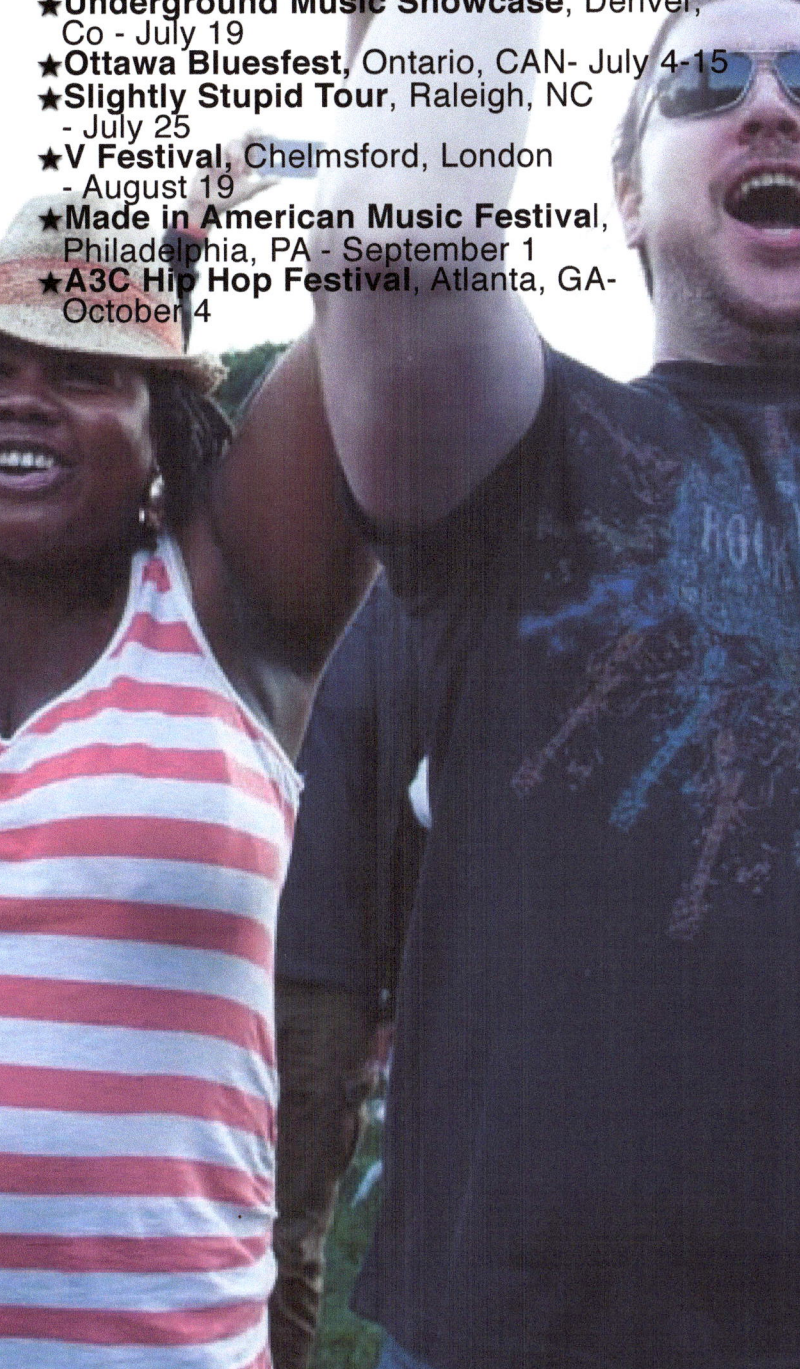

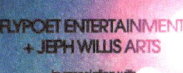
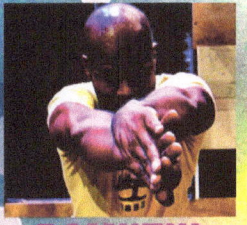
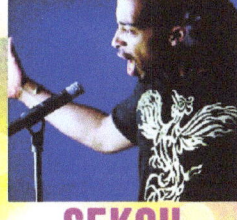
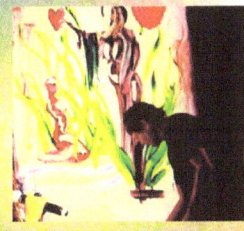
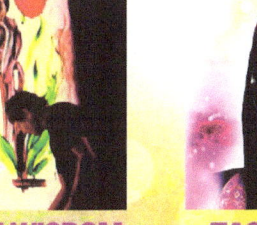
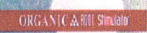 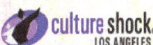 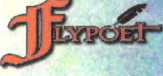

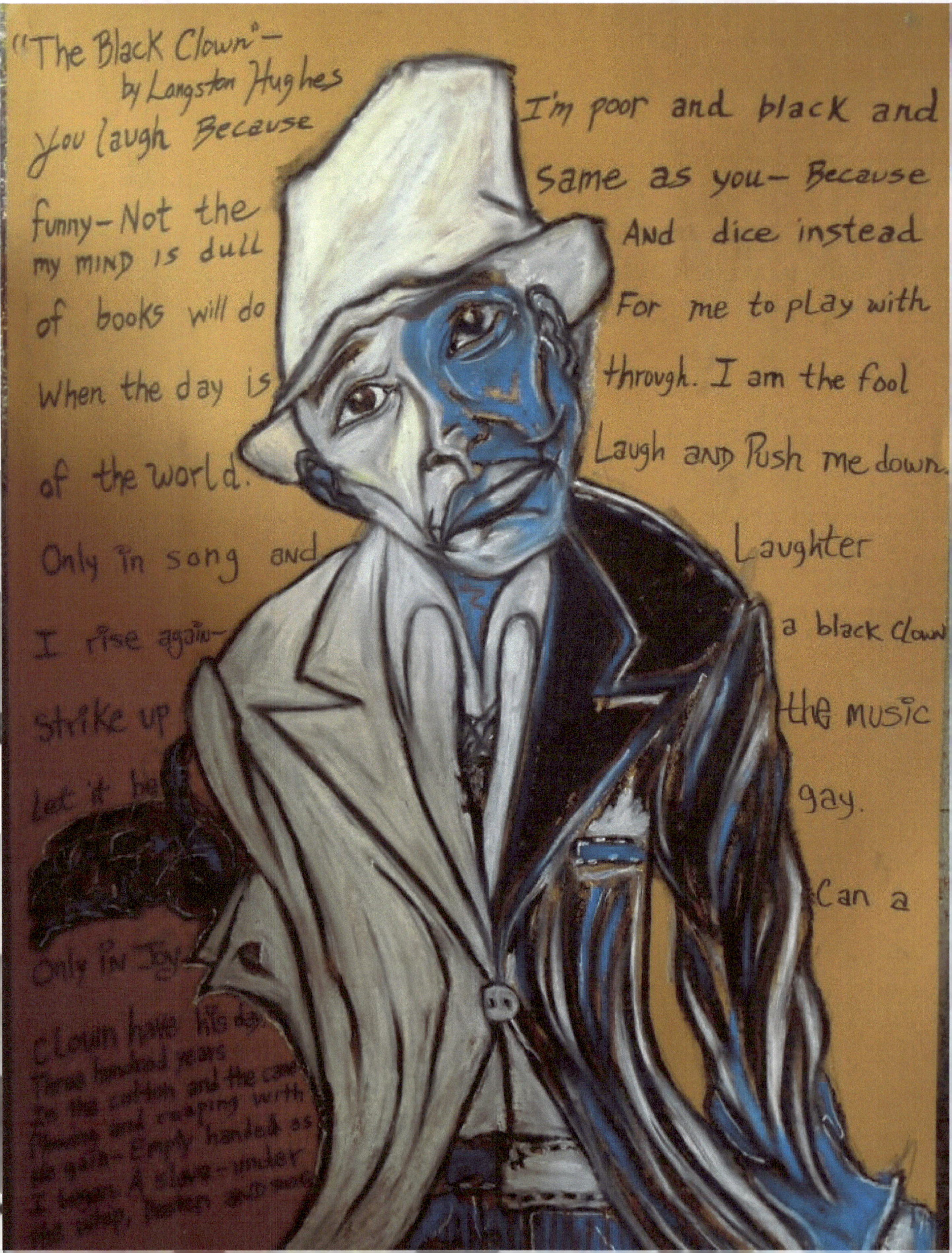

"The Black Clown" —
by Langston Hughes
You laugh Because

I'm poor and black and

funny — Not the
my mind is dull
of books will do
When the day is
of the world.

same as you — Because
And dice instead
For me to play with
through. I am the fool
Laugh and Push me down.

Only in song and

Laughter

I rise again —

a black clown

strike up

the music

Let it be

gay.

Only in Joy

Can a

Clown have his day.
Three hundred years
In the cotton and the cane
and camping with
and again — Empty handed as
I began. A slave — under
the whip, beaten and told

Text by Anthony Thompson Adeagbo.
Visual Art by Renaldo Davidson.

Art TRIBE

LANGSTON HUGHES:

THE BLACK CLOWN PERFORMANCE ART EXHIBITION

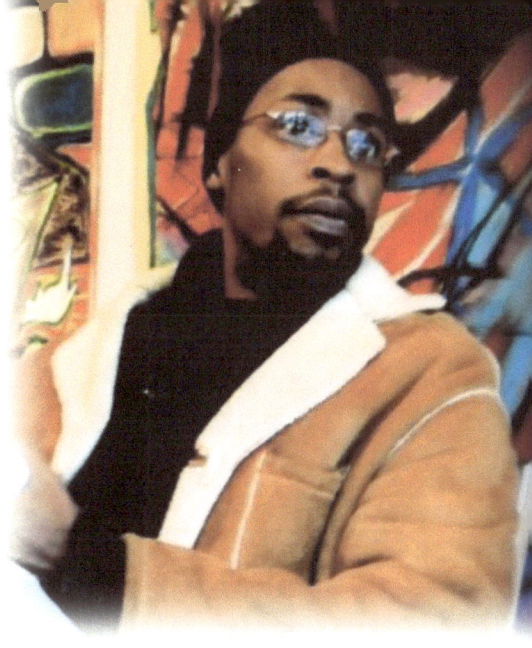

Renaldo Davidson

Langston Hughes lived with strong racial pride and was unashamedly black at a time when blackness was démodé. His work explored the conditions of his people who lived, worked, and survived in spite of great adversity. Langston Hughes' poetry and fiction focused on the working class and everyday ordinary African-Americans. "My seeking has been to explain and illuminate the Negro condition in America and obliquely that of all human kind."A "people's poet," Hughes confronted racial stereotypes, protested social conditions, and sought to uplift his people.

In the new work from Anthony Thompson Adeagbo and Renaldo Davidson, entitled **Langston Hughes: The Black Clown Performance Art Exhibition**, an arrangement of Hughes' dramatic monologue, The Black Clown, is performed by Adeagbo in collaboration with Renaldo Davidson's exhibition of visual pieces inspired by Hughes' monologue, the life of Bert Williams, and Abbey Lincoln's poem, Where Are The African Gods?.

The Black Clown struggles to strip himself of racial stereotypes and social standards placed on him by

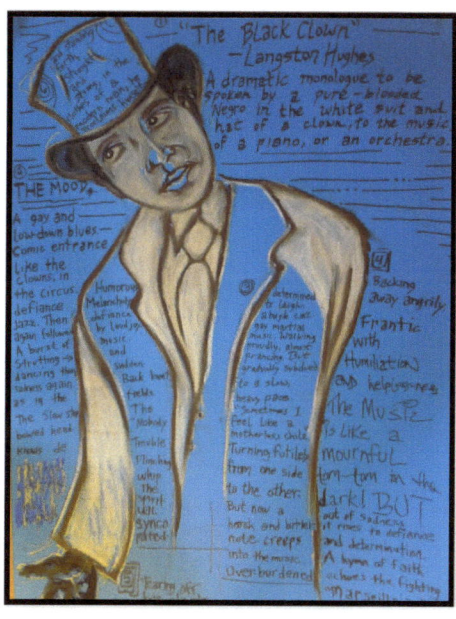

society. Three hundred years working in cotton fields have left him badly damaged by enslavement. Once set free, he has nowhere to go, no money, no job, and must use his hands to free himself from the limitations created by **Jim Crow**. His spiritual transformation reconnects him to his African heritage, allowing him to live with pride and dignity.

Freeing himself from self-hatred, the Black Clown transforms into a man.

Artwork in his exhibition is a multimedia presentation full of vibrant oil pastels that give life to Adeagbo and Davidson's shared interpretations of iconic works. "I try to capture the complexities of our historical social and political existence. It is my hope that my work can help restore the humanity lost of African people through enslavement, racism and oppression," reflects Davidson.

Anthony Thompson Adeagbo and Renaldo Davidson are co-founders of **The Langston Hughes Cultural Enrichment Movement** in Bronx, New York. "Langston Hughes: The Black Clown Performance Art Exhibition is their artistic collaboration. **Visit facebook.com/ hughesenrichment** ∎

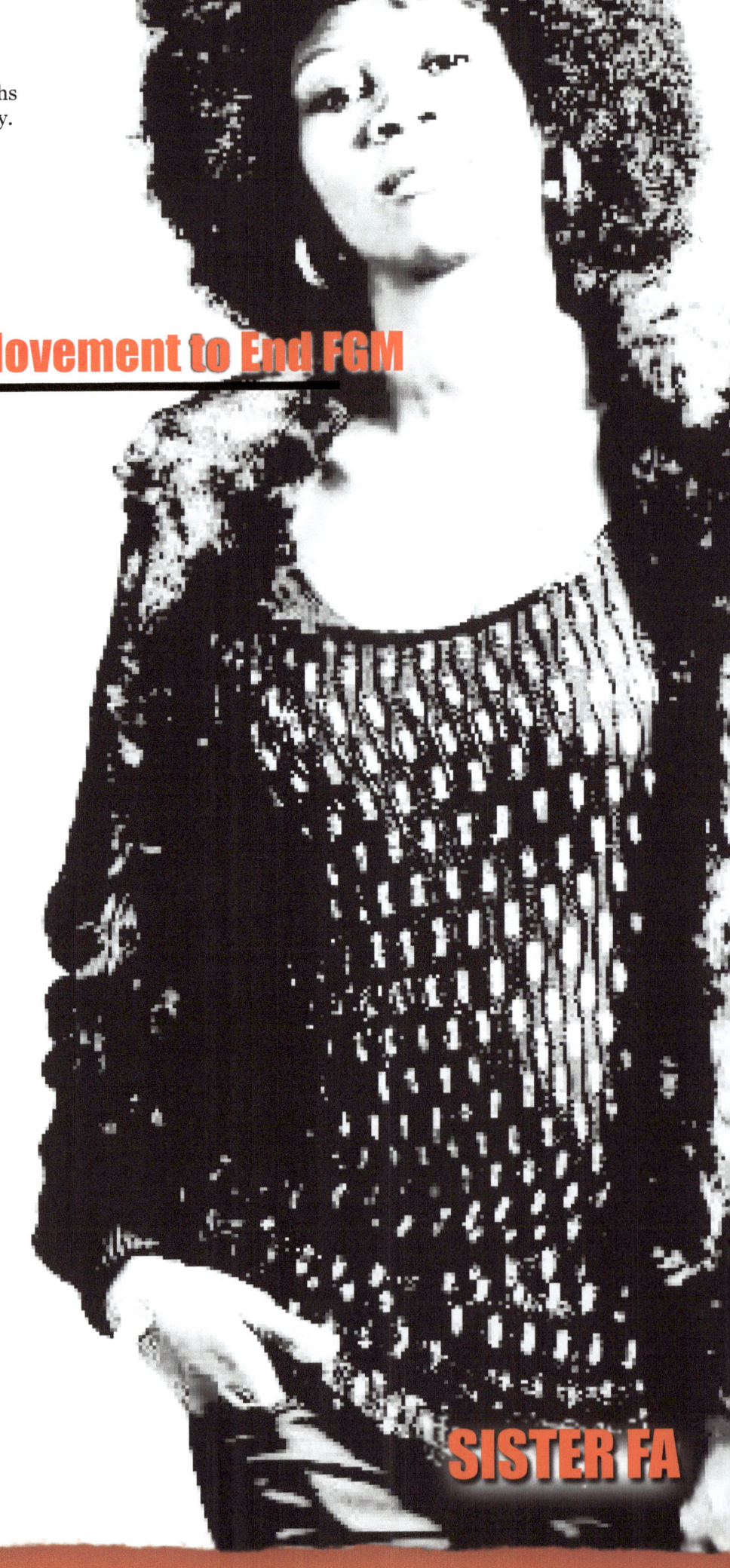

Text by Azra for Patheos.com. Photographs from facebook.com/sarabah.documentary.

Film TRIBE

Sarabah:
Sister Fa and the Movement to End FGM

Sarabah follows the life of Senegalese rapper Fatou Mandiang Diatta, better known as Sister Fa, and her quest to address female genital mutilation (FGM) in her village in Senegal. After releasing her first album and marrying a German PhD student, she found herself in Germany working on her music and wanting to commit to raising awareness of **FGM in Senegal**, as she herself had undergone the procedure as a child.

Sister Fa's organization, **Education Sans Excision**, works with the **NGO Tostan** in advocating for ending the practice. I looked at how Tostan was portrayed in Nicholas Kristof and Sheryll WuDunn's Half the Sky a couple of years ago, and noted the lack of African women's perspectives on FGM in the book. **Sarabah** offers an important personal perspective from a thoughtful, talented African woman.

Tostan's educational emphasis does not aim to vilify the practice outright, and instead promotes a more nuanced discussion of its social necessity, in some instances,

SISTER FA

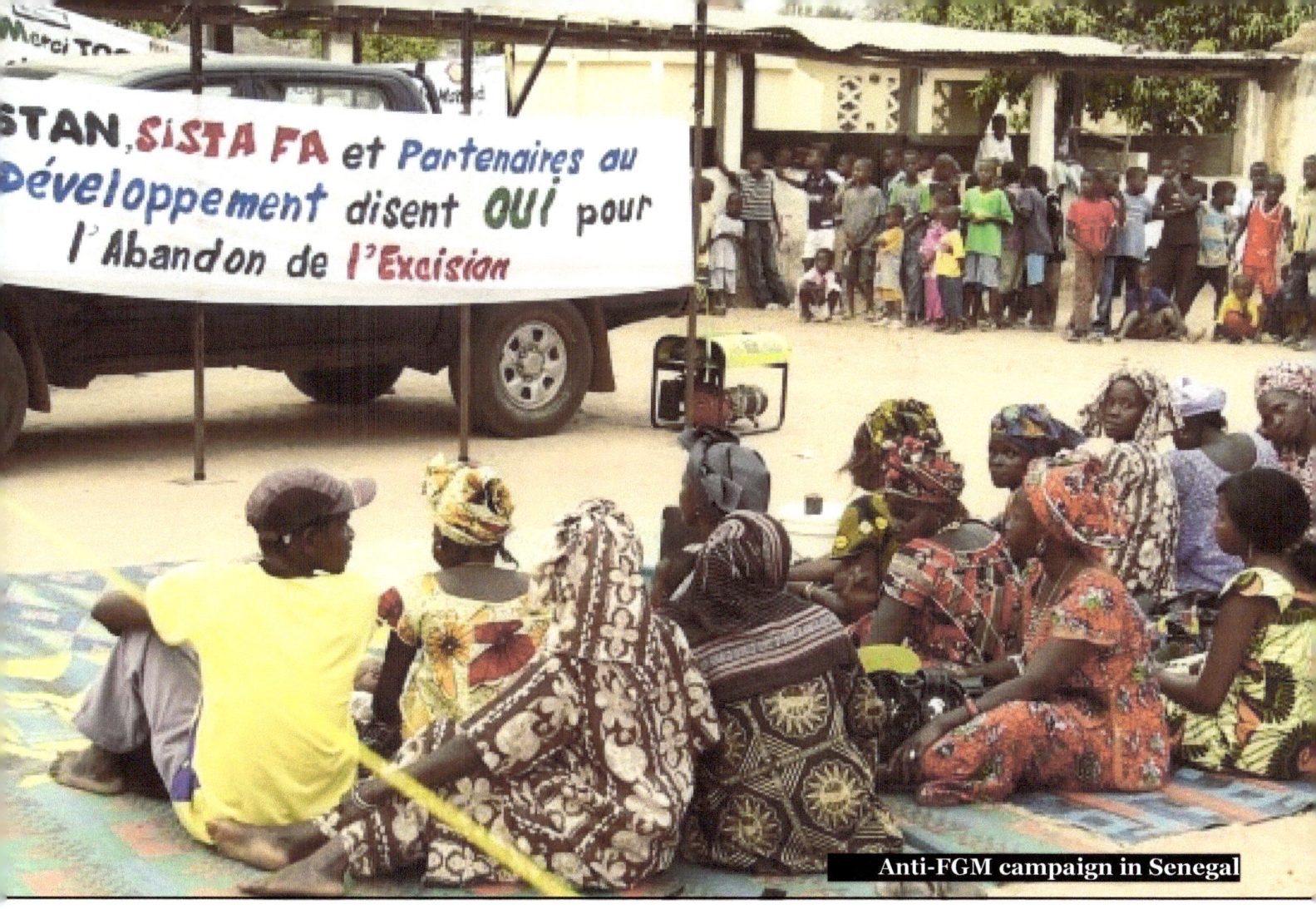

STAN, SISTA FA et Partenaires au Développement disent OUI pour l'Abandon de l'Excision

Anti-FGM campaign in Senegal

as it argues against the practice due to its negative consequences for women's health. Sister Fa adopts this model in her own advocacy work in the country. In an opinion piece for The Guardian last month, Sister Fa relates her complicated understanding of her own experience:

"For years, I wondered why my mother had allowed this to happen. It was not until someone explained to me that she didn't have a choice: she was not cutting me to harm me, but because she felt that she was doing what was the best for me."

When she returns to her village in Senegal with her German band, **Sister Fa** relates how the practice has little to do with Islam. Her village was one of the last to convert to the religion and retains cultural

practices that predate their conversion. Imams might speak for or against the practice according to their own convictions, but it is ultimately women themselves who make the decision for their daughters to undergo the procedure due to its social convention.

Sister Fa is aware of her outsider status as a German resident, and fears being perceived as such as she promotes her anti-**FGM campaign in Senegal**. This discussion is an ever-important one in the field of development—who has the authority to conduct advocacy against harmful social practices? And also: what role might those who have left their countries have to play in promoting wide-scale social change back home? What role do artists play in activism? I was not expecting these points to come up in the film, and found

them refreshing to hear from Sister Fa herself.

In a memorable scene from the film, she is at a primary school near her village, where she engages with students to discuss what FGM is, why it is practiced, and how it is harmful to women's health. At the end of their discussion, they sing a song alongside musicians from Sister Fa's band against excision in their communities. While she also engages in discussion with elderly women in her village, I found it encouraging to see children – both young men and women – having these frank discussions in the same room and later advocating for ending the practice.

Sarabah is an inspiring film, an important viewpoint from the perspective of an African woman who underwent the procedure.

SARABAH FILM

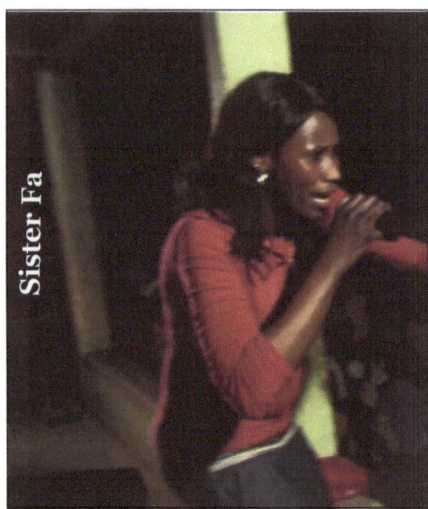

Sister Fa

She reminded me, at times, of the protagonist in **Ousman Sembene's** film, Moolade and the role that media plays in encouraging change. Like the protagonist in that film, Sister Fa does things her own way with resolve and stands firm in her convictions, in both her decisions to pursue a career in music and to return to Senegal for advocacy. Music is a powerful vehicle for discussion. Near the end of her piece in The Guardian, she says:

"I am just trying to speak for the many women who cannot raise their voices. I feel that when I talk, one person listens; but when I sing, thousands of people can hear my song."

To view the trailer, visit sarabah documentary.com. ∎

Poem by Rachel L. Smith.

Poetry TRIBE

Virgin-Slut

Lord,
I know that I am
the first word;
But most people call me
by the second;
Not because of any hard facts;
But instead because
of word of mouth.
A mouth that I would not
let kiss me,
at the end of a date.
My first day ever.
On my sixteenth birthday
Because that is when my parents
said that I could.

All we did;
was sit on the stoop,
watching people walk by.
Only leaving each other-
To talk to friends
who just happened to come by-
and to take a breathe before we
both passed out.

I told my friends
that he was a perfect gentleman.
They knew.
Because they were there.
He told his crew
that I let him touch me,
in places that my mother told me
was mine to wash and keep
clean;
But was never to use it to get or
keep a man.
I should not use it until my
wedding night.
Because once I give it away;
I could not get it back.
My eyes dripped for the entire
day at school.
Like the faucet in my kitchen,
but without the brown sludge.

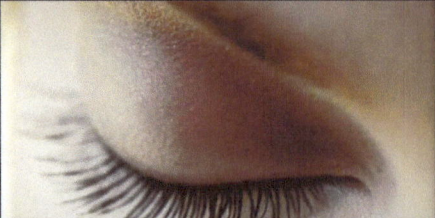

From both the looks and names
that I was called,
and from what my mother/father
would think.

-That Evening-

I walked in the door;
heading straight to my room,
when I heard a familiar voice-
from behind the shut door at the
end of the hall-
ask: "Did you do it?"
"No." I answered whispered.
"That is all I need to hear."
I smiled as I shut the door to my
room.
Mom/dad believed me;
And God knew the truth.

Rachel Smith is a 48 year old single mother. She hopes to spread the message of the power of prayer can have on everyday life. Rachel's poems and writings have been published in Nomad's Choir, Spotlight on Recovery and The Cleveland Chronicle. Visit Rachel's blog at triantic.blogspot.com. ∎

POETRY NEWS!
TRIBES MAGAZINE
has been nominated
"Poetry Magazine of the Year"
by the 2012 National
Poetry Awards! Visit
nationalpoetryawards.com
to learn more!

TRIBES Magazine is
seeking poetry! Submit
your poetry,prose and haikus
to whatsup@
tribesmagazine.com.

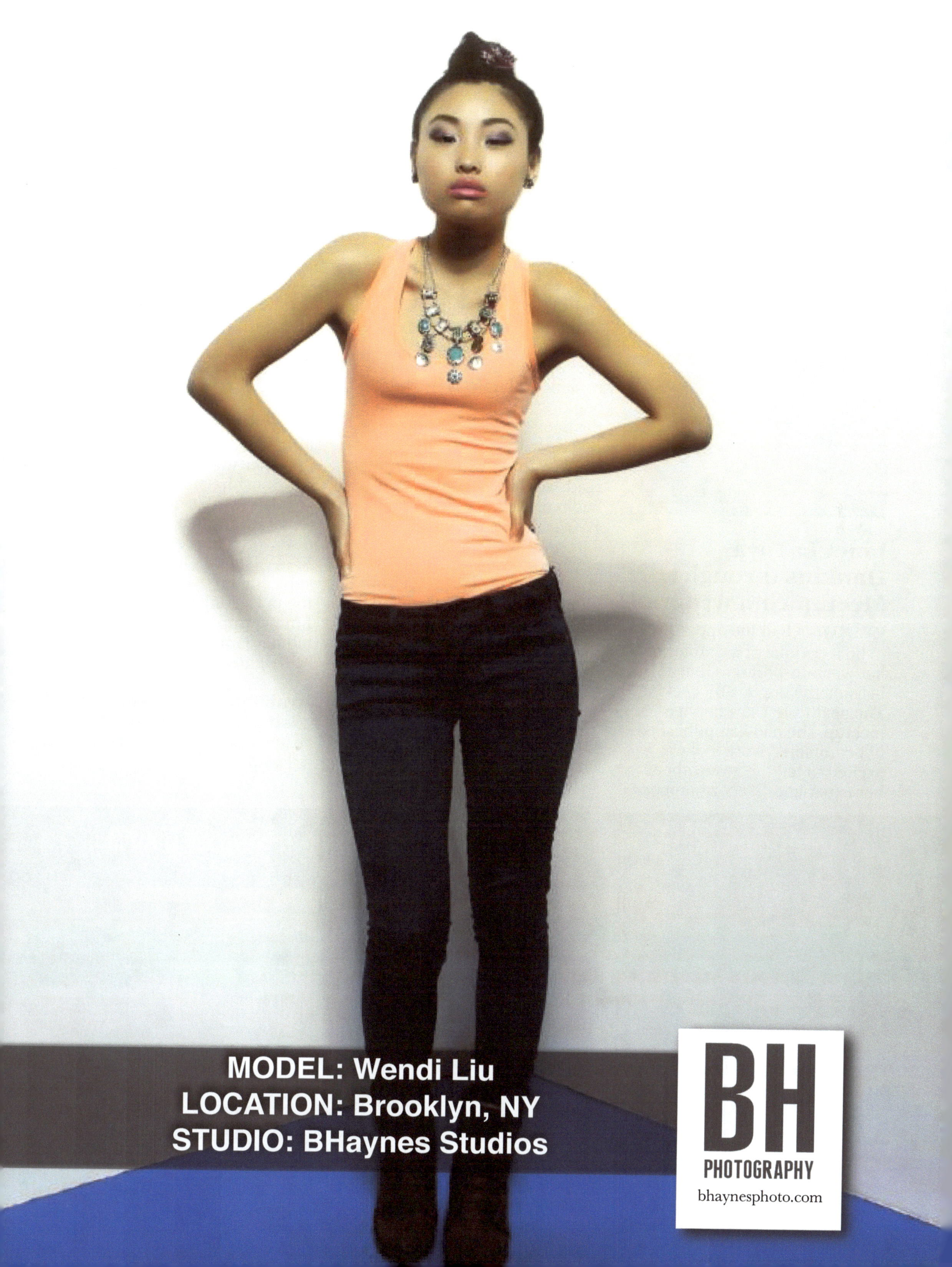

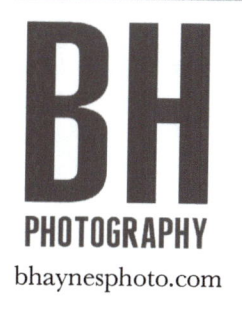

MODEL: Wendi Liu
LOCATION: Brooklyn, NY
STUDIO: BHaynes Studios

BH
PHOTOGRAPHY
bhaynesphoto.com

Text by Sarah Weathersby.
Photographs courtesy of LaToya Hankins.

SBF SEEKING...

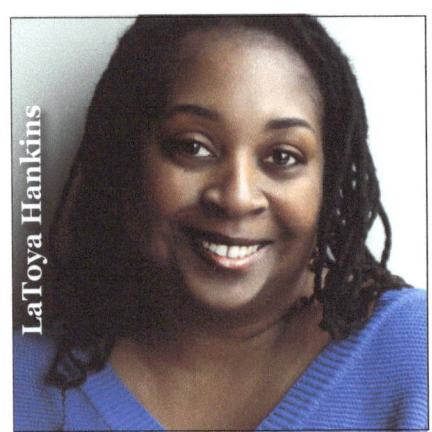

LaToya Hankins

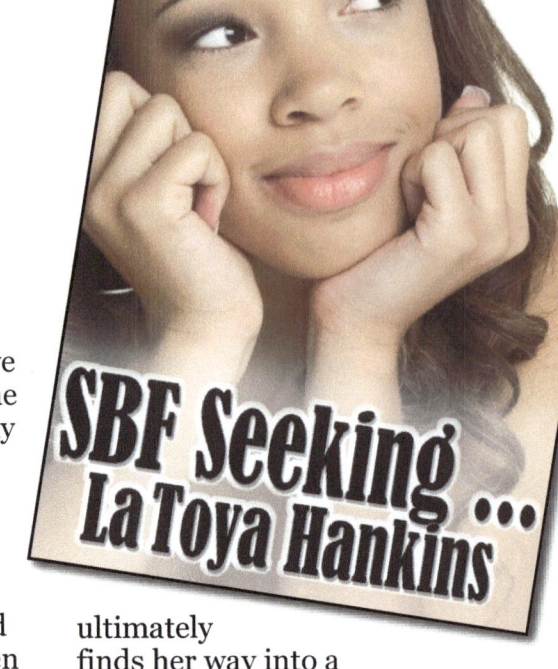

SBF Seeking...
LaToya Hankins

I met LaToya Hankins through a Meetup.com writers group. I had the opportunity to do a critique of a chapter of her work-in-progress that became the novel, SBF Seeking. The next time I saw her at a meetup, she had just published her completed work and was excited to tell the group about her experience. I try to support the talented authors I know, and even though I gave positive and supportive feedback for the chapter I read, I was torn in my reaction, knowing that SBF Seeking was a lesbian romance. Should I buy the book?...Of course. Will I read the book?...Maybe. Then she asked me to write a review and so I had to tell her: I don't often read "gay" literature though I had recently read Justin Torres' *We the Animals* and a couple of James Baldwin books forty years ago.

LaToya was gracious and tried to let me off the hook but I got my hands on the ebook Sample on Kindle and the story grabbed me; a light-hearted romance about a young woman preparing to marry her college sweetheart when she realizes he is not The One. After trying her hand at personals ads and dating other men, she ultimately finds her way into a relationship with a woman and struggles with coming out of the closet when she has only just discovered her sexuality.

Hankin handles the subject matter with humor and the protagonist's experience is a funny ramp until she decides to tell her family; and then the self-righteous bigotry flies.

Available on Amazon.com. Visit googereads.com for more reviews (Search *SBF Seeking*). ∎

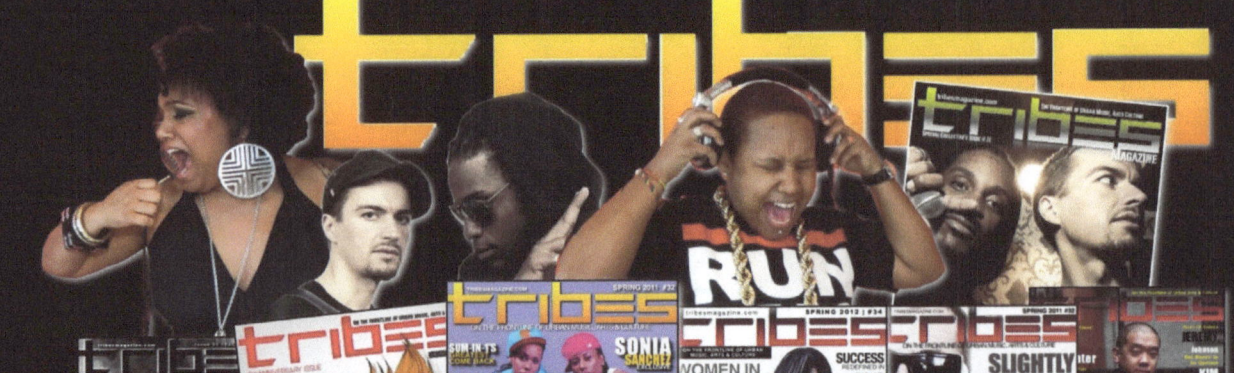
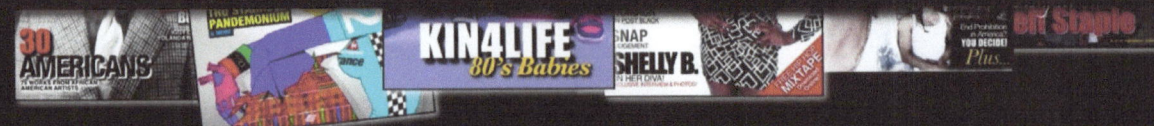

CHECK OUT THESE 2012 SUMMER EVENTS!

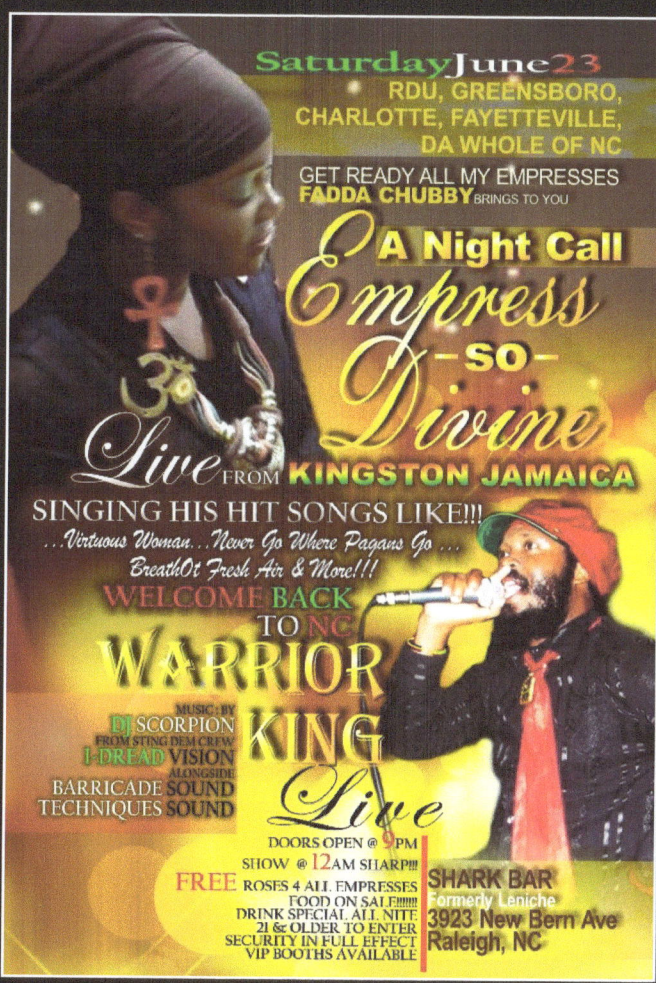

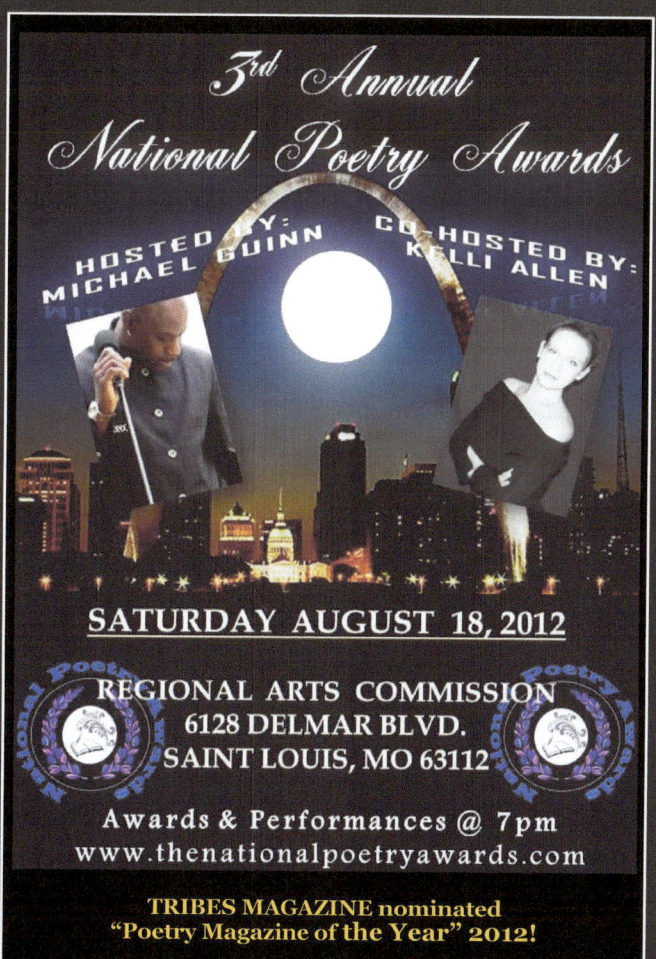

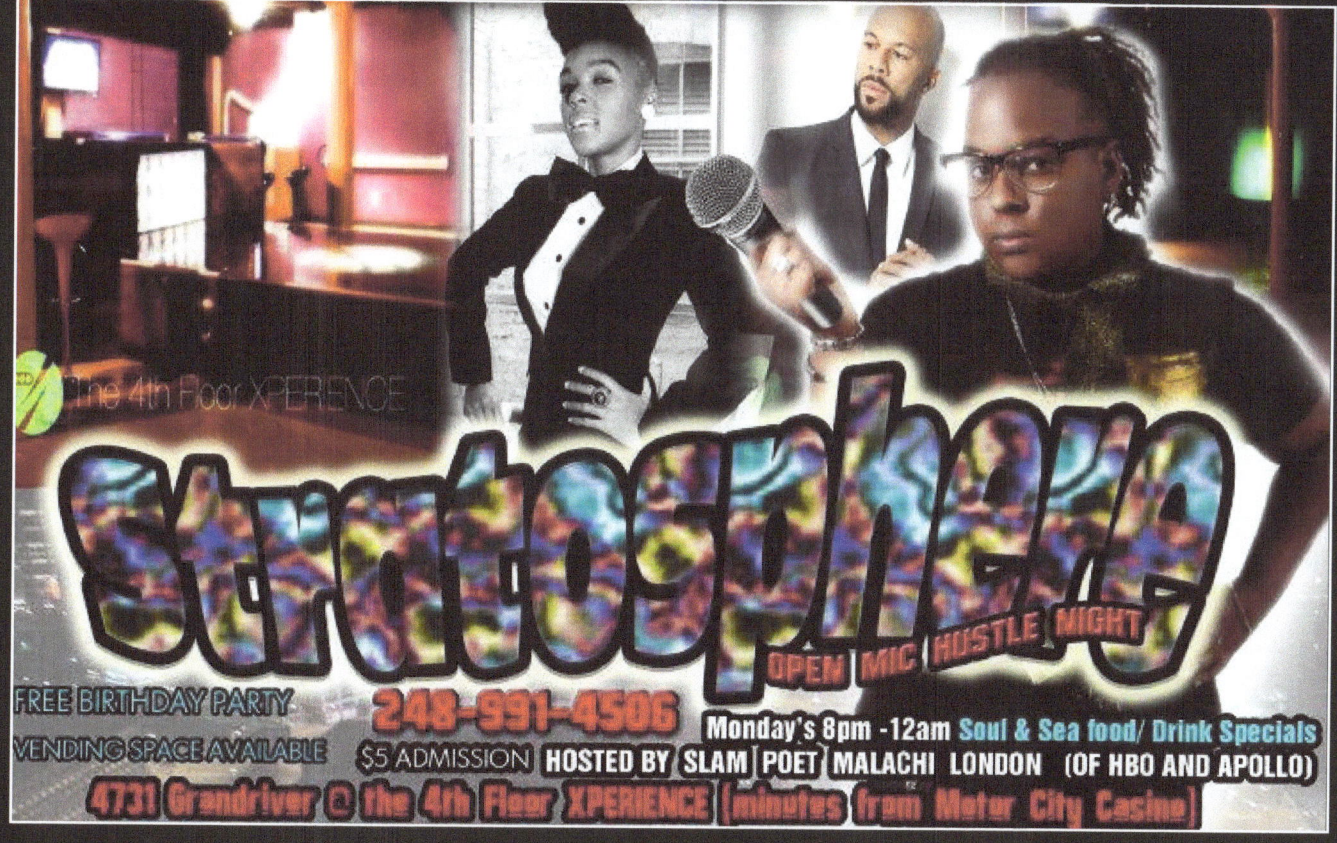